PARTICLE
ACCELERATORS

**DAVID E.
NEWTON**

PARTICLE

ACCELERATORS

FROM THE
CYCLOTRON
TO THE
SUPER-
CONDUCTING
SUPER
COLLIDER

FRANKLIN WATTS · 1989 · A VENTURE BOOK
NEW YORK · LONDON · TORONTO · SYDNEY

Library of Congress Cataloging in Publication Data

Newton, David E.

Particle accelerators : from the cyclotron to the superconducting
super collider / David E. Newton.
p.   cm. — (A Venture book)
Bibliography: p.
Includes index.
Summary: Examines the types, functions, and basic principles of
particle accelerators, both linear and circular, and their
application in the search for the basic building blocks of nature.
ISBN 0-531-10671-3
1. Particle accelerators—Juvenile literature.   [1. Particle
accelerators.   2. Particles (Nuclear physics)]   I. Title.
QC787.P3N48   1989
539.7'3—dc19   88-31375   CIP   AC

Dedicated to
David Parr,
who taught me
what friendship
really means

Diagrams by Vantage Art

Photographs courtesy of:
Stanford Linear Accelerator
Center: p. 26;
Fermilab: pp. 31, 57, 58;
Photo Researchers: pp. 61 (SPL),
63 (David Parker/SPL);
NASA: p. 97.

CONTENTS

PARTICLE
ACCELERATORS

CHAPTER ONE

A HALF-CENTURY OF PARTICLE ACCELERATORS

The moment was one of high excitement for M. Stanley Livingston. A turn of the dial would soon tell this graduate student in physics if he was to make scientific history. His advisor, Ernest O. Lawrence, had proposed this machine as a way of breaking apart atomic nuclei. But would the idea actually work in practice?

Livingston turned the dial and . . . success! The machine worked. The world's first circular particle accelerator, or cyclotron, was in operation.

This historic scene took place on the Berkeley campus of the University of California in early 1932. The cyclotron opened a new era in our study of the atom.

During the first two decades of the twentieth century, scientists had made enormous strides in learning about the atom. They had found that atoms consist of two parts: a dense, positively charged core called the nucleus, surrounded by negatively charged particles called electrons. They had also discovered some basic facts about the way electrons behave.

But by the late 1920s, the atom's nucleus still remained an intriguing mystery. Scientists had discovered one component of the nucleus, the positively charged proton. They also suspected the existence of a second, uncharged particle. This particle, the neutron, was discovered somewhat later, in 1932. But little else about the internal structure of nuclei was known.

The problem was that very large amounts of energy were needed to break apart the nucleus in order to find out what was inside. In 1919, the English physicist Ernest Rutherford had used high-energy particles from naturally radioactive materials to blow apart the nuclei of atoms. But this technique had only limited usefulness. Only a minute number of nuclei could be broken apart by this process. What was needed was some kind of machine that could accelerate particles fast enough so that they could collide with large numbers of atoms and break apart their nuclei.

Lawrence's cyclotron was just such a machine. But it was not the first particle accelerator to have done so. Only months before the Berkeley success, a somewhat similar experiment had been conducted in Great Britain. Working in the famous Cavendish Laboratory at Cambridge University, the English physicist John Cockroft and his Irish colleague E. T. S. Walton had successfully tested their own type of particle accelerator, a straight-path, or linear, accelerator.

When fast-moving protons from the Cockroft-Walton machine collided with a target made of lithium metal, nuclei in the lithium atoms disintegrated. The proof that disintegration had occurred was that helium, which is lighter than lithium, was observed among the products of the reaction. For the first time, humans had found a way to blow apart atomic nuclei with a machine.

Progress in machine design • Both the Cockroft-Walton machine and the Lawrence cyclotron made possible some exciting discoveries in particle physics. But both machines became obsolete within a few years. Only a limited amount of new information could be obtained with the energy provided by the machines. When that information had been collected, the machines could provide no new discoveries. Further progress in studying atomic nuclei required larger machines with greater amounts of energy.

And that pattern has been repeated again and again for the past half-century: New machines yield exciting new discoveries, become obsolete, and are replaced by larger, more powerful machines. As a result, the machines in use today are so big and so powerful that they make the original Cockroft-Walton and Lawrence accelerators look like peashooters.

The largest linear machine today, for example, is three thousand times longer and one hundred thousand times more powerful than the first Cockroft-Walton accelerator. The most powerful circular accelerator in operation today produces proton beams with one million times the energy of those produced by Lawrence's original cyclotron.

Designing today's most powerful accelerators involves new, difficult technological problems, however. One doesn't get a more powerful machine simply by making the older model twice or three times as big.

For example, when particles begin to move very fast, their mass begins to increase. The faster that protons and electrons move in an accelerator, the heavier they get. As they gain mass, they then begin to slow down. Factors such as this one are the kinds of problems accelerator designers have to take into account as they build larger and larger machines.

Colliders and fixed-target accelerators • The last decade has also seen a shift toward colliding-beam rather than fixed-target accelerators. In a fixed-target machine, like the Cockroft-Walton or Lawrence accelerators, a fast-moving beam of particles smashes into a piece of material at rest. Most of the beam energy in this kind of machine is lost in moving atoms in the target and is not useful for experiments that a physicist might want to conduct.

In a colliding-beam machine, two beams of particles going in opposite directions smash into each other. All of the energy from both beams is available for experiments. This improvement is important because a major objective of particle, of high-energy, physics is to create new particles.

Colliders are therefore much more desirable machines, but they are also much more difficult to build and use. In fact, particle accelerators for scientific research have become so large, so complicated, and so expensive that few are built anymore. In the 1950s, more than a hundred particle accelerators were in operation in the United States alone. They were even considered to be common equipment in university physics laboratories.

By the late 1980s, however, less than a dozen large accelerators were available worldwide for high-energy research in physics. Only four such machines were in operation in the United States.[1] Each machine costs tens or hundreds of millions of dollars to build and millions more to operate. Each requires a staff of thousands of scientists and technicians to keep it running. The operation of accelerators has become, therefore, one of the most massive economic projects in all of science.

A never-ending conquest of the nucleus • Yet, the need for particle accelerators has not diminished. Physicists have learned a great deal about the basic structure of matter using these machines. Dozens of subatomic particles—particles smaller than atoms—have been produced by blowing nuclei apart.

These particles often have strange names—kaon, pion, and W boson—and even stranger properties. For example, many survive only a few billionths of a second after being created in the collision.

One of the great achievements of modern physics has been the development of a theory that makes sense out of the host of particles discovered in accelerator experiments. This theory, called the Standard Model, explains how three of the four basic forces of nature—the electromagnetic, weak, and strong forces—are related to a handful of truly fundamental nuclear particles.

Still, particle accelerators have furnished physicists with no "final" answers about the composition of matter. The Standard Model is as much a guide to future experiments as it is a way of summarizing what we already know about the structure of matter.

Each new machine answers some of the questions physicists have asked but also provides new and unexpected data leading to still more questions. Even as they solve some old problems, experiments with accelerators lead to more basic, even more interesting, problems and questions.

The latest step in this process, in the evolution of particle accelerators, is a machine known as the Superconducting Super Collider, or SSC. In the planning stages for nearly a decade, the SSC will be the world's largest particle accelerator when it is completed in about 1996. The ring, in which protons will be accelerated to energies twenty million times as great as those of the first cyclotron, will have a diameter of 26 kilometers (16 miles) and a circumference of about 83 kilometers (52 miles)!

Planning for the SSC has been carried out by a group of scientists organized by the Universities Research Association, a group of fifty-six universities in twenty-six states and the Canadian province of Ontario. The United States government will pay expected construction costs of at least $4.4 billion and annual operating expenses of about $270 million.[2] Japan and European nations may also contribute to the cost of building and operating the SSC.

Scientists expect the SSC to teach them even more about the nature of matter. They expect to carry out further tests for the Standard Model of matter. They hope that results of SSC experiments will answer some of their questions about the origin of the universe. But, more than anything, they will expect surprises, new discoveries, unexpected events that may conceivably call for an even larger, more powerful particle accelerator in the future.

Principles of particle acceleration • To some extent, the story of particle accelerators is all about a single law of physics. That law says that particles with like electric charges repel each other and particles with unlike electric charges attract each other. In the first place, the law explains why it is that we even need particle accelerators in order to break apart nuclei. Imagine trying to hit an atom with a slow-moving particle carrying a negative electric charge. That particle will be deflected by electrons in the target atom. Or imagine trying to hit the atom with a slow-moving particle carrying a positive electric charge. That particle will be deflected by the nucleus of the target atom. In either case, one way to overcome the force of electrical repulsion is to make the moving particle go *very fast*. Then, it has enough energy to collide with and break apart the nucleus.

Particle accelerators are designed to make use of the same law of electrical attraction and repulsion. Suppose that an electron is placed between two electrically charged plates, one charged positively and one charged negatively. The space between the charged plates constitutes an electric field because any charged particle placed within that space feels a force of attraction or repulsion. In this case, the negatively charged electron will be repelled by the negative plate and attracted by the positive plate.

The pull toward one plate and push away from the other plate causes the electron to move. The stronger the charge on the plates, the faster the electron can be made to move. Even with two very highly charged plates, however, an electron does not gain enough energy to penetrate a nucleus.

That result can be achieved by having the electron pass through a *series* of charged plates. Within the gap between each set of plates, the electron gets an additional kick, raising its velocity each time. Eventually the electron is going fast enough to penetrate an atomic nucleus.

This accelerator design works for any charged particle. As long as a particle carries a positive or negative charge, it can be accelerated by charged plates. Most particle accelerators use protons, electrons, positrons (positively charged electrons), or antiprotons (negatively charged protons) as their bullets.

Neutrons are not used in particle accelerators. They would certainly make good bullets. Since they carry no charge, the neutrons would not be repelled by an atom's electrons or by its nucleus. In theory, even a slow-moving neutron could easily smash an atom. The problem is how to get a neutron or any other neutral particle moving at all. The usual method of accelerating particles described above doesn't work with neutral particles. Placed between positively and negatively charged plates, a neutral particle remains at rest.

Measuring particle energy • Physicists usually talk about the final *energy* of a beam, rather than its final velocity. Energy and velocity are closely related to each other, since the energy of a beam depends partly on its velocity.

The energy of particle beams is usually measured in some multiple of electron volts. An electron volt (abbreviated as eV) is the amount of energy gained or lost by an electron as it passes through an energy field of 1 volt.

That's about the amount of energy an electron gets by traveling from one end of a flashlight battery to the other.

The most common measures of accelerator-beam energy are as follows:

kiloelectron volts (keV), or thousands of electron volts

megaelectron volts (MeV), or millions of electron volts

gigaelectron volts (GeV), or billions of electron volts

teraelectron volts (TeV), or trillions of electron volts

So that you have something to compare, the first Cockroft-Walton linear accelerator produced an energy beam of 500 keV; the first Lawrence cyclotron, a beam of 1 MeV; the largest existing linear accelerator, a beam of about 50 GeV; and the proposed SSC, a beam of about 20 TeV.

CHAPTER
TWO

LINEAR
ACCELERATORS

A linear accelerator (often referred to simply as a linac) consists of hundreds or thousands of hollow tubes arranged in a straight line (Figure 1). Particles are injected at one end of the machine, accelerated through the tubes, and directed at a target at the end of the machine. Exiting particles collide with and break apart nuclei of atoms in the target material.

The particles most commonly used in linacs are protons or electrons. Protons are obtained from hydrogen gas. Hydrogen atoms consist of only a single proton and a single electron. Removing electrons from hydrogen gas, then, leaves a supply of naked protons. Electrons are produced simply by heating a wire very hot. Electrons "boil off" the hot wire and enter the accelerator at the source.

To understand how a linear accelerator works, as-

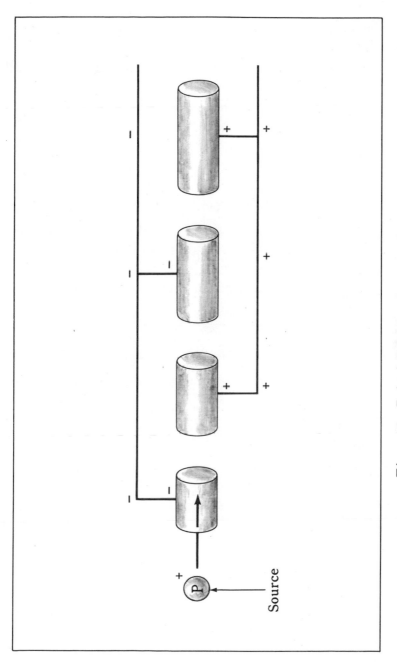

Figure 1. Principle of the linear accelerator

sume that we want to accelerate protons. Each of the tubes that make up the linac carries an electrical charge. When the machine is turned on, the first, third, fifth, and every other odd-numbered tube is charged negatively. The second, fourth, sixth, and every other even-numbered tube is charged positively.

A proton emitted at the source is attracted to the first tube. It moves toward and then into the tube. Once inside the tube, the proton no longer experiences any electric charge. (The electric charge on a hollow object is located only on the outside of that object and exerts no effect on anything inside the object.) The proton simply keeps moving—"drifting"—through the tube. For that reason, the tubes are sometimes known as drift tubes or cavities.

As the proton passes through the first drift tube, however, a critical change takes place. The electric charge on the first and every other drift tube reverses. Every positively charged tube becomes negatively charged, and every negatively charged tube becomes positively charged.

Thus, the proton reaches the gap between the first and second drift tubes and "sees" a positively charged drift tube behind it and a negatively charged drift tube in front of it. The proton is repelled by the tube it just left and attracted to the tube next in line. This gives the proton a kick in the forward direction.

The proton is already in motion when it receives this second kick, so it moves even more rapidly through the second tube than it did through the first.

Timing is crucial in this process. The electric charges on the drift tubes have to change at just the right moment, not a fraction of a second too soon or too late.

Most of us learned this principle (without knowing it) during childhood. That lesson came on playground swings where we learned how to make a swing go higher and faster. The technique was to have a friend give the swing a push at just the right moment. If the push came at the highest backward point in the swing's arc, the swing continued to go higher and faster. If it came too soon or too late, the swing slowed down instead of speeding up. The same is true in getting electric charges to change at precisely the right moment in a linac.

You can probably guess what happens when the proton reaches the gap between the second and third drift tubes. The electric charge on all the cylinders changes again, back to the condition when the proton first entered the linac. The proton gets a third kick forward and picks up even more speed.

This process continues again and again, as many times as there are drift tubes in the machine. Finally, when the proton has passed through the final cylinder, after a journey of less than a millisecond (thousandth of a second), it smashes into a target at the end of the machine.

Interior of the linac • The interior of a linac that accelerates protons looks different from one used to accelerate electrons. In a proton linac the drift tubes are not all the same length. Instead, each tube, going from source to target, is a little longer than the preceding one. Here's the reason for that design.

The electric charge on the drift tubes in the machine changes regularly, say, 200 million times every second. That means a drift tube will be positively charged one instant, negatively charged one-200 millionth of a second later, positively charged one-200 millionth of a second after that, and so on.

That pattern is fine if the proton reaches each succeeding gap in exactly the same time. But it doesn't. It keeps going faster and faster as it passes down the machine. It might take a billionth of a second to go through the first drift tube, but only a millionth of a second to go through the fifth, for example. Soon the proton will get "out of phase" with the alternating charges on the cylinders. It will arrive before the charge has changed and will not get the kick it's supposed to.

To compensate for this increase in speed, designers build the drift tubes longer and longer, going from one end of the machine to the other. Every time the particle speeds up, it has a longer distance to travel, and it arrives at the next gap just in time for the charge change.

Electron linacs do not have this feature. The electrons that enter a linac reach nearly the velocity of light after traveling the first meter or so of the machine. After that, their velocity is constant (nearly the speed of light) along the rest of the machine. Since they travel the same distance in the same time along each drift tube, the tubes can all be the same length.

Electron linacs do not even need drift tubes. Instead, they can use washerlike disks that carry an electromagnetic wave through the linac. The electrons ride on the crest of the wave, like a surfer on a water wave. The disks match the speed of the electromagnetic wave to that of the electrons, causing the particles to be accelerated continuously throughout the machine.

Finally, in either a proton or an electron linac, the whole series of drift tubes is enclosed within a larger tube. All the air has been removed from the drift tubes and the enclosing tube. If air remained in the drift tubes, electrons or protons in the particle beam would collide with air molecules and be scattered and lost. This principle is, in fact, a general one. The working parts of all particle accelerators are always enclosed within a vacuum.

The maximum speed achieved by a particle in a linac depends on the number of drift tubes in the machine. A particle that gets kicked through a hundred drift tubes will end up moving faster than one that goes through only fifty drift tubes. The secret to making a powerful linac, then, is to make it as long as possible.

Of course, like almost any project, the engineering problems involved in building a linac get much more difficult as the machine gets larger. One problem in building an accelerator 100 kilometers (60 miles) long, for example, would be that the particle path would no longer be a straight line but would follow the curvature of the earth.

The Stanford Linear Accelerator Center (SLAC) • Construction on the Stanford Linear Accelerator Center (SLAC) linac was begun in 1962 and completed four years later. An underground tunnel 3 kilometers (2 miles) long contains the 82,650 accelerating cavities and magnetic, electrical, and auxiliary equipment needed in the machine. Electrons accelerated in SLAC's linear accelerator attain a maximum energy of about 32 GeV.[3]

A critical problem in construction of the SLAC linac was the alignment of the accelerating cavities. Over a distance of 3 kilometers, factors such as the earth's cur-

vature can cause minor but significant variations in the position of the drift tubes. This problem was solved by attaching a laser beam to the linac itself. As each section of the linac was installed, the laser beam was used as a guide to obtain precise alignment. The method was highly successful. The completed linac shows a deviation of no more than 0.005 centimeter (0.002 inch) over its entire length.

Three new machines have been installed at SLAC in the last two decades. In each one, electrons are caused to collide with positrons in a large ring. The first collider, nicknamed SPEAR, is a ring 80 meters (260 feet) in diameter attached to the linac. Some electrons from the linac are bent in one direction around the SPEAR ring (Figure 2). Other electrons are used to make positrons, which are then accelerated in the opposite direction. Electron-positron collisions in SPEAR yield an energy of about 8 GeV.

The success of SPEAR led SLAC physicists to design a larger machine of the same type. This ring, called PEP, has a diameter of 800 meters (2,600 feet) and produces beam collisions of 40 GeV.

The tunnel housing the linear accelerator at Stanford University can be seen in this aerial photo. The two-mile (3-km) long accelerator runs under Interstate Highway 280 south of San Francisco.

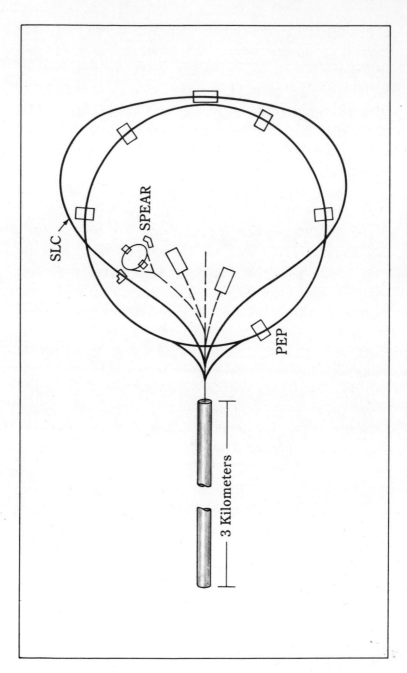

Figure 2. Accelerators at the Stanford Linear Accelerator Center

The latest expansion of the colliding beam concept at SLAC is called the SLAC Linear Collider (SLC). SLC has dimensions about the same as those of PEP but will attain energies close to 100 GeV.

SLAC has been the site of some major advances in particle physics, including the discovery of two new subatomic particles, the tau lepton in 1975 and the psi (now called the J/psi) in 1974.

Particle detectors • Blowing atomic nuclei apart with a linac is only part of the job. More work needs to be done after the particle beam collides with the target. Next, the researcher has to find out what happened as a result of the beam-target collision.

To answer that question, physicists have designed a variety of particle detectors. A particle detector is any device that provides information about the properties of particles produced during a collision. All particle accelerators have particle detectors. Most particle detectors make use of a common physical principle. When a rapidly moving particle passes near an atom, the particle strips one or more electrons from the atom. The electrically neutral atom is replaced by two charged particles—a negative electron and a positively charged ion. The process is called ionization. Any device that can detect the electrons or the ions formed during ionization can recognize the passage of the particle.

Such a device is the bubble chamber. A bubble chamber consists of a tank that contains a pure liquid. Liquid hydrogen, helium, xenon, propane, and freon are all commonly used in bubble chambers.

The liquid is heated to a temperature above its boiling point (at normal atmospheric pressure), but it is prevented from boiling by the application of pressure on the liquid. Thus, liquid hydrogen normally boils at $-252°C$ ($-422°F$), but in a bubble chamber it is usually warmed to about $-245°C$ ($-409°F$). To prevent the hydrogen from boiling, a pressure of 540 kilonewtons per square meter (78 pounds per square inch) is applied to the liquid.

In the instant before particles pass through the bubble chamber, the pressure on the liquid is reduced and the liquid is ready to boil. Any particle that passes through the chamber will (1) ionize hydrogen atoms in the liquid and (2) release a tiny bit of energy in the process. At each point where ionization occurs, a tiny bit of liquid boils and changes to a gas, forming a single small bubble in the process. The path of the particle can be traced by following the string of bubbles that form in the liquid.

Cameras surrounding the bubble chamber record these tracks at the instant they form. Within moments, the whole container of liquid boils and must be restored to its original superheated condition as quickly as possible.

Detection devices such as the bubble chamber may be surrounded by a magnetic field. The magnetic field causes particles that pass through the detector to travel in curved lines. Scientists can determine a particle's charge, mass, and velocity by the size and shape of its "footprint" in the bubble chamber (Figure 3).

Another detection device is the calorimeter, a device that measures the energy of a particle, a material, or a reaction. A particle produced within an accelerator, for example, may fly out of the machine and into a calo-

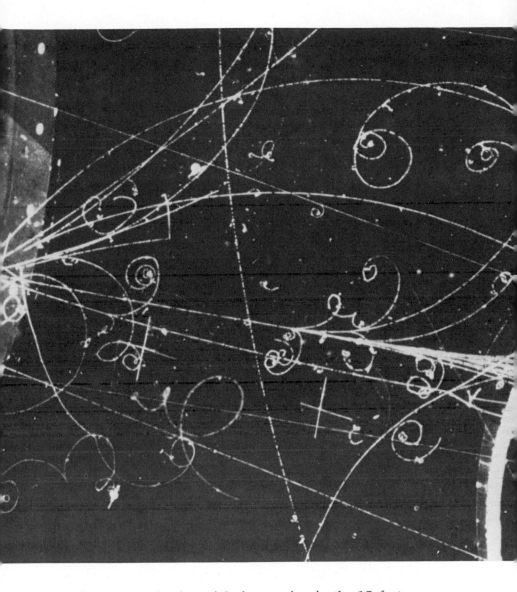

A photograph of particle interaction in the 15-foot (4.6-m) bubble chamber at Fermilab in Batavia, Illinois. The photographs showing particle "tracks" are studied by scanners and experimenters.

rimeter detector. Within the detector, the particle smashes into a target, converting its energy of motion into heat energy. The amount of heat produced in the calorimeter tells how much energy the particle had when it left the accelerator.

Another detecting device makes use of Cherenkov radiation. Cherenkov radiation is a faint bluish glow produced when rapidly moving particles pass through glass, liquid hydrogen, liquid carbon dioxide, water, or other transparent materials. The effect depends on the relative speed of light in such materials.

You probably know that nothing can move faster than light in a vacuum. But the same cannot be said for materials other than a vacuum. For example, very fast electrons can and do move faster than light when passing through glass. The fast-moving electrons produce an effect like a shock wave, which produces the bluish Cherenkov effect. Cherenkov radiation can be used in particle detectors because the angle with the particle's path at which the radiation is given off is determined by the velocity of the particles that caused the radiation. By measuring this angle of exit, physicists can calculate the speed of particles that passed through the detector.

Spark chambers, multiwire counters, and drift chambers operate on a common principle. All contain thin metallic wires or plates surrounded by a gas inside a box-like container. The wires or plates are electrically charged. When a particle passes through one of these chambers, it ionizes the gas. Electrons and other charged particles produced during ionization travel toward the nearest wire or plate. Movement of the electron or charged particle is then magnified by the charge on the wire or plate, producing a kind of "cascade" effect that can be recorded and studied. In the spark chamber, for example, the voltage on plates is high enough to cause sparks to form along the trail of ionized particles. By arranging many wires or plates within a chamber, the pathway followed by the particle can be charted.

Most accelerators use a combination of these detectors. One type may be used to determine the energy of particles produced in the machine, a second to determine the particles' velocities, and a third to determine their charge.

CHAPTER THREE

CIRCULAR ACCELERATORS

One possible disadvantage of linacs was apparent to the earliest accelerator designers: linear accelerators had the potential to become very long machines. Thus, while some particle physicists were working on linear accelerator design, other physicists were taking another approach. They were building machines in which particles travel in circles.

In a cyclotron, a charged particle moving at a right angle to a magnetic field travels in a circle (Figure 3). The radius of that circle depends on four factors: the mass, charge, and velocity of the particle and the strength of the magnetic field.

Suppose we talk about accelerating protons. The mass and charge of the proton are normally constant. (At very high speeds the proton's mass changes, but we'll deal

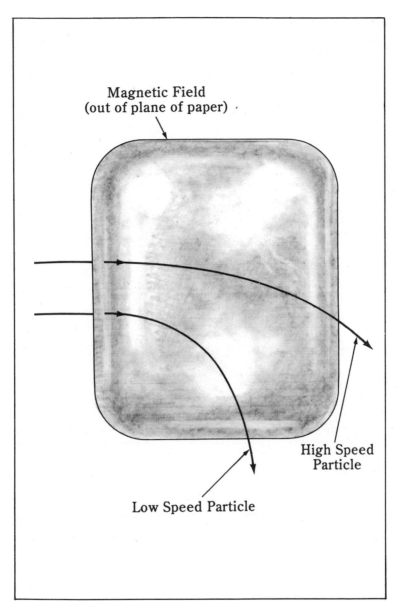

*Figure 3. Path of a charged particle
in a magnetic field*

with that problem later.) So the radius of the proton's circular path depends only on its speed and on the strength of the magnetic field. Specifically, the radius of that circle gets larger as the velocity of the proton increases, and the radius of the circle gets smaller as the strength of the magnetic field increases. These physical principles provide a basis for accelerating particles in a circle rather than in a straight line.

How a cyclotron works • A cyclotron consists of two hollow half-cylinders. If you cut a cat food can down the middle, you would have something that looks like the first cyclotron ever built. Each half of the can has the shape of the letter D (Figure 4). The halves are, therefore, called "dees." The dees are connected to a source of radio frequency alternating current, assuring that they always carry opposite charges. When one dee is positive, the other is negative. The rate at which the current changes, known as the frequency of oscillation, is typically about ten million times per second.

Large magnets are positioned above and below the two dees. The magnets are much larger than the dees themselves. They are arranged so that a magnetic field passes vertically through the dees, from one magnet to the other.

To understand how the cyclotron works, assume that we want to accelerate protons. The protons are injected at the center of the machine, in the gap between the two dees. At the moment the protons appear in the gap, they are repelled by the positively charged dee and attracted to the negatively charged dee. They move out of the gap and into the negatively charged dee. Since they are mov-

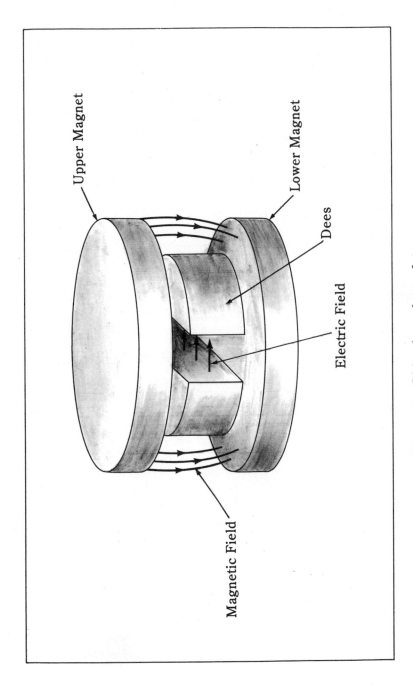

Figure 4. Side view of a cyclotron

ing through a magnetic field, however, they travel in a circular rather than a straight path.

Inside the dee, the protons continue to travel in a circular path. Eventually they leave the dee and re-emerge in the gap between the dees. At just this instant, the electric current has reversed. The positively charged dee becomes negatively charged, and the negatively charged dee becomes positively charged. The protons in the gap between dees are repelled from the dee they have just left and pulled into the opposite dee.

As protons enter the second dee, they are moving faster because of the kick they got in the gap. Thus, they're moving in a circle of larger radius in the second dee. As they emerge from that dee and enter the gap again, the current has reversed once more. The protons are accelerated into the first dee and travel in a still larger circle. The whole process continues again and again until the protons' path reaches the outer edge of the dees. On their final trip, they exit through a window in the wall of the cyclotron and collide with the target material (Figure 5).

Keeping the alternating current in step with the protons is made easy by the laws of physics. The protons travel faster and faster during each trip around the cyclotron. But the path they travel is also longer on each trip. Early on, the protons move quite slowly, but the arcs they travel are small. Later the protons are moving much faster, but they are then following much larger arcs.

These two factors—faster velocity and longer path—compensate for each other. Thus, the time it takes a proton to make a trip around the cyclotron is, with exceptions to be mentioned later, always the same. The times required to make the first, second, eighth, and

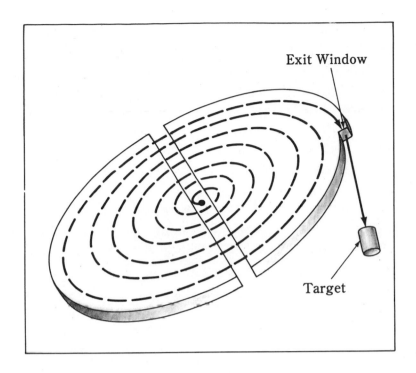

Figure 5. Path of a proton in a cyclotron

hundredth trip are identical to each other, and the proton gets to the gap just as the current changes.

What happens in a cyclotron is similar to what goes on in a linac. The kick that protons get between dees is like the kick particles get in the gap between drift tubes in a linac. The difference is that the magnetic field of a cyclotron makes the particles move in a curved path (a circle) rather than in a straight line. As particles speed up in a linac, they travel through longer and longer drift tubes. As particles speed up in a cyclotron, they travel in larger and larger arcs.

Ernest O. Lawrence's first cyclotron was a modest

device made of coffee cans, sealing wax, and leftover laboratory equipment. It measured only 11 centimeters (4.3 inches) in diameter and produced protons with only 80 keV of energy. Based on the success of this model, however, he was able to get a grant of $1,000 from the National Research Council to build a larger machine. The second accelerator was 25 centimeters (9.8 inches) in diameter and produced the first million-electron-volt particle beam in 1932.[4]

Cyclotron development • Building a more powerful cyclotron might seem to be a simple task. By increasing the diameter of the dees, particles would have a greater distance to spiral out; they would have more revolutions from which to pick up additional energy. That approach was followed for a while. Lawrence and Livingston built a 69-centimeter (27-inch) cyclotron in 1933 and upgraded it to 94 centimeters (37 inches) in 1936. The largest cyclotrons ever built were a 218-centimeter (85.8-inch) cyclotron at Oak Ridge National Laboratory, and a 225-centimeter (88.6-inch) machine at the Nobel Institute in Stockholm, both built many years later. These two cyclotrons could accelerate protons to energies of 22 MeV.[5]

The most popular cyclotron design uses a somewhat smaller diameter, about 150 centimeters (59 inches). Machines of this size were built and operated at the University of California at Berkeley in 1939 and, after World War II, at the Brookhaven and Argonne National Laboratories.

Unfortunately, the idea of simply making a cyclotron larger and larger doesn't work out in actual practice. Other physical laws make it impossible to expand cyclotrons to unlimited sizes by the straightforward method described here. Larger accelerators can produce higher energy levels, accelerating particles to higher velocities. But at velocities close to the speed of light a particle's mass begins to change. Its circular path in a cyclotron is now dependent on a third factor, its mass, in addition to its velocity and the strength of the magnetic field. This change places a limit on the size of the traditional cyclotron—about 20 MeV—and necessitates modifications in the design of more powerful circular accelerators.

Synchrocyclotrons • In 1905, Albert Einstein showed that when a particle begins to move, it gains mass. (The term "mass" refers to the amount of material an object contains and is closely related to the term "weight." "Mass" is the preferred term to use, however, because it is more precise.)

The mass of a proton is usually given, for example, as 1.67×10^{-24} (0.000 000 000 000 000 000 000 001 67) grams. What we are really referring to in this statement, however, is the proton's mass when it's not moving, its rest mass.

When the proton begins to move, however, its mass increases. At low velocities, this increase is small. A particle moving at one-fifth the speed of light (60,000 kilometers, or 37,000 miles, per second), for example, has a mass only 2 percent greater than its rest mass. But particles in even a small accelerator move *very* fast, often close to the speed of light (300,000 kilometers, or 186,000 miles, per second). At these speeds, the mass increase (called the relativistic mass increase) is significant.

The problem that this change creates is that the

proton begins to slow down as its mass increases. That means that the time required for the proton to make a trip around the cyclotron will not be the same each time, but will get longer and longer with each trip.

One way to deal with the problem of relativistic mass increase is to adjust the frequency of the electric current that drives the particles so that the particles will arrive at the accelerating gap (between drift tubes or between dees) at the exact moment required for them to get the next kick in their onward path.

To illustrate this method, consider the motion of a proton in a cyclotron. By the time a proton has made many trips around the machine, it's moving at velocities near the speed of light. As a result, its mass has increased significantly.

Imagine what effect this has as a proton approaches the gap between dees on, say, its hundredth trip around the cyclotron. The proton, now heavier than it was before, moves more slowly and therefore takes longer to complete a circle in the machine. It will not reach the gap between the dees as quickly as it had on previous revolutions. When the charges on the dees reverse, the proton will not be in position to get the next kick in its onward movement. Instead, it will get a kick in the wrong direction or will feel no kick at all.

When this happens, the system used to speed up the proton has now begun to backfire and is slowing the particle down rather than speeding it up.

One obvious solution to this problem is possible. Normally, the electrical charges in a simple cyclotron reverse at a regular rate. But suppose this pattern were to be changed. Suppose the rate at which the electric field changes slows down over time. In such a case, the electric field could be made to reverse a bit later than it had on earlier revolutions. In a sense, the electric field would "wait" for the more massive proton to get to the gap. When the field did reverse, it would do so with the proton in just the right position for the next kick.

The modified cyclotron described here is called a synchrocyclotron. In a synchrocyclotron the frequency of the electric field is synchronized with the relativistic mass changes in the particles as they revolve in the machine. The names "frequency-modulated (FM) cyclotron" or, in the Soviet Union, "phasotron" are also sometimes used for this machine.

Modulating the frequency in a synchrocylotron changes the way particles are delivered by the machine to the target. In a cyclotron, particles enter the machine and then are accelerated in bunches. Bunching occurs because half the time the charge on the dees is of the wrong sign to accelerate the particles. In a synchrocyclotron, bunching occurs differently.

Imagine a bunch of protons that enter a synchrocyclotron at the instant the machine is turned on. That bunch of protons will be accelerated around the machine and gain mass, as described above. As the protons gain mass, the machine frequency decreases so as to stay in phase with this bunch of protons. The frequency continues to decrease, staying with the particles until they have completed their journey through the machine and have been delivered to the target.

But now imagine a second bunch of protons that enter the machine just after the first bunch of protons. At the instant the second bunch enter the synchrocyclotron, the frequency of the machine is being tuned to the first bunch of protons. The frequency can't stay in phase with both the first and second bunches of protons at the same time. The second bunch will be out of phase with the machine frequency. They will have to wait until the frequency returns to its original value, or they will just be lost within the machine. In the latter case, they will never travel through the machine or be delivered to the target. The same can be said for the third, fourth, fifth, and many other bunches of protons that enter the machine shortly after the first bunch. In fact, about 99 percent of all the protons that enter the machine will be out of phase with the current machine frequency and will be lost. Only those protons that enter the machine at the instant the frequency returns to its original value will be able to make their way through the synchrocyclotron.

As a result, the way particles are emitted from a synchrocyclotron is different from the way they leave a cyclotron. In the latter case, particles leave the machine in a stream of bunches, each bunch containing about half of all particles injected into the machine. Particles also leave the synchrocyclotron in a stream of bunches except that each bunch contains only about 1 percent of all particles that originally entered the machine.

The first synchrocyclotron was put into operation at the University of California at Berkeley in November 1946. The 467-centimeter (184-inch) machine used equipment originally intended for a large standard cyclotron before Lawrence discovered that he could not overcome the effect of relativistic mass increase with traditional methods of cyclotron technology, namely through the use of higher and higher dee voltages.

Over the next decade, synchrocyclotrons were also constructed at a number of locations around the world, including Dubna, in the Soviet Union (1954, 467 centimeters/236 inches); Geneva (1958, 498 centimeters/196 inches); the University of Chicago (1951, 432 centimeters/170. inches); and the University of Liverpool (1954, 396 centimeters/156 inches).[6] About twenty synchrocyclotrons worldwide are currently in operation.

Synchrocyclotrons are capable of accelerating protons to energies ranging from 100 MeV to about 1 GeV. The upper limit of 1 GeV for synchrocyclotron proton beams comes from the cost of the magnets used for such machines. While the magnets for a 180-centimeter (72-inch) synchrocyclotron weigh about 200,000 kilograms (200 tons), those for a machine less than four times as large would weigh fifty times as much, or about 11,000,000 kilograms (11,000 tons).[7] At this larger size, it's less expensive to go to another type of cyclotron than it is to make bigger synchrocyclotrons.

Sector-focusing cyclotrons • A second solution to the problems caused by relativistic mass increase exists. Instead of modulating the electric fields, one can change the magnetic field. Recall that the radius of a particle's circular path in an accelerator depends, among other factors, on the strength of the magnetic field. A stronger magnetic field reduces the radius of the circle traveled by the particle. Imagine once more a bunch of protons that have traveled a hundred thousand times around a cyclotron and increased in mass. Again, the protons slow down and fail to reach the gap when the current changes direction.

But now suppose that the magnetic force on the particles is increased. A stronger magnetic force means the particles will travel in a smaller circle. Since they travel in a smaller circle, they do not have as far to go. It takes less time for them to travel along the smaller circle than it would have to travel along the larger circle. They are able to get to the gap on time as the current changes.

Again, though, nature doesn't allow us to get away with a solution quite that easily, for when the magnetic field is increased on the particles, they tend to drift upward and downward, away from the center of the beam. Instead of reaching the exit port as a sharply defined, pencil-shaped beam, the particles get all "fuzzed out" and arrive as a broad smear. They are useless for experimental purposes in this shape.

An ingenious solution to this problem was worked out by Llewellyn H. Thomas at Ohio State University in 1938. Thomas showed how to increase the magnetic field on the revolving particles and at the same time to keep them from drifting away from each other. The solution was to divide each dee into pie-shaped wedges and alternate the magnetic field strength (strong-weak-strong-weak) within the wedges. This technique, known as sector-focusing, is now a standard feature in most new cyclotrons.

Synchrotrons • Synchrotrons represent the next stage in the development of particle accelerators. The great majority of the world's most powerful accelerators today are synchrotrons. A synchrotron combines many of the principles developed in the cyclotron, the synchrocyclotron, the sector-focusing cyclotron, and the linear accelerator.

Particles enter a synchrotron (Figure 6) having al-

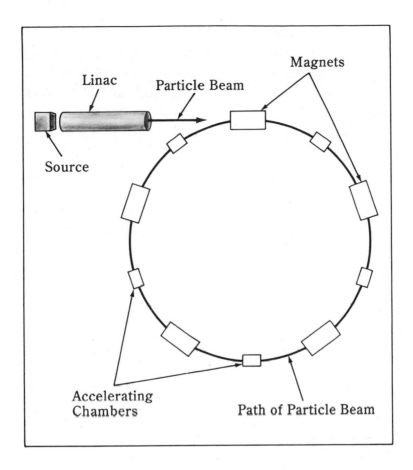

Figure 6. Plan of a synchrotron

ready been accelerated to a high speed in a smaller accelerator, commonly a linac. In an electron synchrotron, electrons almost always enter the machine moving at essentially the speed of light. For example, an electron with only 2 MeV is already moving at 98 percent the speed of light.[8]

In a proton synchrotron, entering protons may be

traveling anywhere from nearly the speed of light to only one-tenth that amount. The variation in initial speeds of electrons and protons is one of the most important differences between an electron synchrotron and a proton synchrotron.

Particles receive additional kicks of energy as they move through accelerating cavities. These cavities may be placed symmetrically along the circumference of the synchrotron, or they may be lined up along only one section of the ring. The cavities act much like the gaps between drift tubes in a linear accelerator. Indeed, the synchrotron ring bears some resemblance to a linac wrapped into a circle.

Typically, a bunch of particles may complete a few thousand to a few hundred thousand revolutions in the second or so they are in the ring. During each revolution, particles in the bunch pick up anywhere from a few keV to a few MeV of additional energy. Particles leaving the ring will have as little as 10 MeV or as much as 1,000 GeV of energy.

The path in which revolving particles move in the synchrotron is carefully controlled by magnets placed along the ring. These magnets act much like those in a sector-focusing cyclotron. As the revolving particles gain energy in the accelerating cavities, the magnetic fields increase in time, forcing the particle beam to remain in a fixed circular path.

The design of a synchrotron represents a technological advance for at least two reasons. First, since a bunch of particles always move along the same path, the chamber in which the particles travel can be as simple as a circular tube. In fact, the particle beam itself may be no more than a few centimeters wide throughout the ring. Second, and far more important; the area over which magnets have to act is relatively small, just the narrow tube through which the particle beam travels. Enormous magnets, like those needed to cover the 467-centimeter (184-inch) synchrocyclotron, are therefore unnecessary. Smaller magnets do the job. Since the cost of magnets is a major expense in the construction of an accelerator, this improvement is a great economic advantage.

Proton and electron synchrotrons are used in similar ways. Both are primarily research instruments used to study the composition of matter. Because protons react with matter somewhat differently from the way electrons do, researchers may prefer one machine over the other for certain specific projects. The release of synchrotron radiation from electron synchrotrons (discussed in the next section) makes these machines useful also for some kinds of practical projects as, for example, in the treatment of certain diseases.

The first electron synchrotron of the type described here came into full energy operation at the University of California at Berkeley in 1949. It produced electron beams of 320 MeV. The first proton synchrotron in operation was the 3-GeV Cosmotron at the Brookhaven National Laboratory. Table 1 shows some of the larger synchrotrons now in use around the world.

The problem of synchrotron radiation • Relativistic mass increase is not the only problem accelerator designers have to think about when particles move very fast. Another factor that needs to be considered is synchrotron radiation. The laws of physics say that any time a charged

Table 1.⁹ Some of the World's Major Synchrotrons

Location	Type	Opened	Maximum Energy (GeV)	Radius (meters)
Cornell University	e	1967	12.2	125
Yerevan, USSR	e	1967	6.1	35
Daresbury, UK	e	1966	5.2	35
DESY, Hamburg, WG	e	1964	7.5	50
Brookhaven, NY	p	1960	33	129
Serpukhov, USSR	p	1967	76	236
CERN, Geneva	p	1976	400	1100
Fermilab, Illinois	p	1972	400	1000

e = electron synchrotron
p = proton synchrotron

particle is accelerated, it will radiate energy in the form of electromagnetic waves (light). In a particle accelerator, that energy is known as synchrotron radiation.

Consider, for example, an imaginary situation in which an electron passes through a linear accelerator. The electron gains energy from the machine and picks up speed as it moves from one end of the linac to the other. Any increase in speed such as this is acceleration.

As long as the electron accelerates in the linac, it loses some energy in the form of synchrotron radiation. At first the electron accelerates slowly and emits only a small amount of synchrotron radiation. The moving electron gains energy from the machine much faster than it loses energy by synchrotron radiation.

If we could imagine accelerating the electron fast

enough, however, it would lose a larger fraction of energy by synchrotron radiation. Eventually a break-even point is reached at which the electron radiates energy away as fast as it gains energy from the machine. There would be no point in adding any more energy beyond this point since the added energy would all be lost as synchrotron radiation and the electron would go no faster.

Our linac example of synchrotron radiation is imaginary since the loss of energy from particles traveling in a straight line is too small to worry about. In even the largest existing linac, synchrotron radiation is an insignificant consideration.

Neither is synchrotron radiation a problem with circular proton accelerators. Particles lose energy by synchrotron radiation faster when traveling in a circle than in a straight line. However, the rate at which a charged particle radiates energy is strongly dependent on the particle's mass. Since the proton is two thousand times as heavy as an electron, it radiates energy much more slowly than does an electron.

But synchrotron radiation *is* a problem with circular electron accelerators. At first glance, one might suppose that it would be possible to make a very large electron synchrotron that could produce 200 GeV, 300 GeV, or even larger amounts of energy. But the existence of synchrotron radiation makes that dream impossible. For, as energy output in an electron synchrotron approaches 10 GeV, particles begin to lose energy as fast as the machine supplies it.

One way to deal with this problem in theory is to build a larger accelerating ring. Machines with a larger radius, that is, that more closely approximate a straight line path, lose energy by synchrotron radiation less rapidly. However, the cost of building bigger and bigger accelerators eventually becomes just too great. Synchrotron radiation places a limit, therefore, on the maximum energy of any electron synchrotron.

For this reason, scientists at first viewed synchrotron radiation as an unpleasant reality of the natural world. It was "unpleasant" because it set a limit on the size of electron synchrotrons. Recently, however, they've begun to find ways of making the best of this physical limitation by finding a number of practical applications for synchrotron radiation. As one example, synchrotron radiation is being used to manufacture some of the smallest electron chips now being produced.

Colliding-beam accelerators • All accelerators described thus far—whether linacs or circular accelerators—share one common problem. When the particle beams they produce strike a fixed target, only a small fraction of the beam's energy can be used in an experiment. The major portion of the energy simply is lost as the target breaks apart.

The reason for this situation is summarized in the law of conservation of momentum. The momentum of a particle is equal to the product of its mass multiplied by its velocity. According to the law of conservation of momentum, the total momentum of all particles in the beam and target before a collision must be the same as the momentum of all particles remaining after the collision.

When particles in a beam collide with a target at rest, their forward momentum has to be conserved. It is conserved by putting into motion pieces of a target produced during the collision. Very little of the energy of the beam particles is left over for creating new particles.

For example, less than 5 percent of a 1-TeV (1000 GeV) proton beam can be utilized to make new particles in an experiment when the beam hits a fixed target. The other 95 percent goes to driving target nuclei forward in the direction the beam is moving. [10]

In contrast, the collision of two beams traveling toward each other releases a great deal more useful energy. In that case, the two beams are traveling in opposite directions (one in a positive direction, the other in a negative direction), and their total momentum before and after collision is zero. Thus, all the energy of both beams can be utilized in an experiment. For example, two 1-TeV beams that collide with each other will release all the energy from both beams (2 TeV) for use in making new particles.

Accelerators that use colliding beams are often referred to as storage rings because the particle beams inside them may travel within the rings for a long time, many hours in some cases. Very precise magnets are necessary to keep the beams in tightly defined, fixed paths. In the case of electron beams, accelerating cavities are also necessary to compensate for energy radiated away as synchrotron radiation while the beams circulate.

The first successful colliding-beam experiment was completed at the Italian National Laboratory at Frascati when a 200-MeV electron beam collided with a 200-MeV positron beam. [11] All of the next generation of particle accelerators being planned and built for research at the forefront of particle physics, including the Superconducting Super Collider, are to be colliders.

The Tevatron at Fermilab • Research at the frontiers of particle physics takes place today at Stanford's linac and a handful of giant synchrotrons around the world (Figure 7). One of these machines is the Tevatron at the Fermi National Accelerator Laboratory (Fermilab). The Tevatron gets its name from the fact that it produces particle beams with 1 TeV of energy, making it the most powerful accelerator in the world.

Protons used in the Tevatron are first accelerated to 8 GeV in three feeder machines—two linacs and a booster synchrotron (Figure 8). Then, they are injected into the accelerator's main synchrotron, whose ring is about 2,000 meters (6,500 feet) in diameter, or 6 kilometers (4 miles) in circumference.[12]

When originally built, the Tevatron used conventional magnets made of steel and copper. Now, a second set of magnets using superconducting coils has been installed and is used to accelerate protons to their maximum energy of 1 TeV. The Tevatron can be operated as either a fixed-target accelerator or as a collider. In the former case, protons leave the main ring and are deflected to one of several research areas. Different kinds of experiments using the 1-TeV beam are carried out in each area.

In order for the Tevatron to operate as a collider, some protons in the beam are used to make antiprotons. The antiprotons are produced in the proton-metal collision that takes place outside the main ring. They are accumulated for about four hours in a separate ring until enough are present to make the antiproton beam useful for experiments. Then the antiprotons are reinjected into the synchrotron, where they move in an orbit opposite

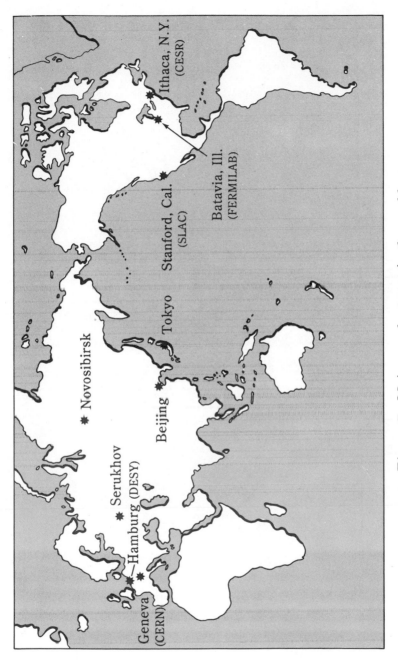

Figure 7. *Major synchrotrons in the world*

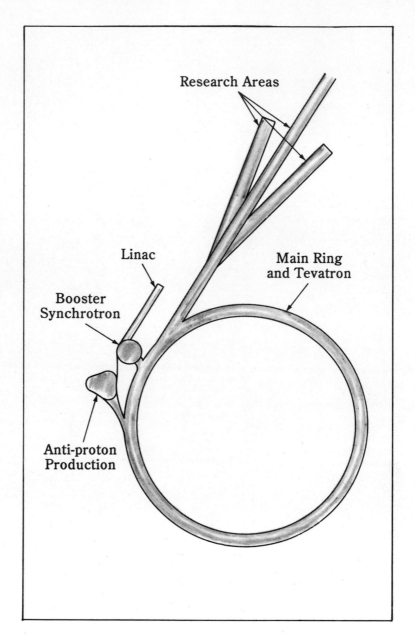

Figure 8. Layout of the Fermilab Tevatron

The most powerful accelerator in the world is the Tevatron at Fermilab.

The tunnel of the main accelerator at Fermilab. The arrow points to the upper ring of magnets which are the 400-GeV accelerator. The lower ring are superconducting magnets for the Tevatron.

to that of the protons, and are accelerated to 1 TeV. At the desired moment, the two beams are made to collide, releasing a total of 2 TeV of energy.

Six positions on the ring have been designated as interaction areas. At all of these points, proton and antiproton beams can be made to collide. Detectors at each location allow scientists to identify and study particles produced in these collisions.

In addition to its work as a research accelerator, the Tevatron has another important function. It has been used to test many of the ideas and techniques on which the SSC design is based. Typical of the new technology used in the Tevatron are the superconducting magnets which are crucial to the eventual operation of the SSC.

Development of the first superconducting magnets for accelerators was started at Fermilab in 1972. (A similar project begun at Brookhaven in 1970 ultimately failed.) The Fermilab project involved the construction of more than two hundred test magnets and took seven years to complete. And by 1983 Fermilab had constructed a thousand more superconducting magnets and installed them in the Tevatron.

Since 1983, the Tevatron has been capable of operating with either conventional or superconducting magnets. Information obtained from research and testing with the accelerator has been invaluable in the design of the SSC. Indeed, one might say that without the experience gained at the Tevatron, the SSC would not have been a realistic concept in the 1980s.

Centre Européen pour la Recherche Nucléaire (CERN)

• A second important synchrotron is located at the Centre Européen pour la Recherche Nucléaire (CERN) in Geneva, Switzerland. The machine was built and is operated by a consortium of thirteen European nations. As far back as 1949 these nations realized that only very wealthy countries, such as the United States and the Soviet Union, could afford to build particle accelerators. So they decided to pool their assets and construct a single machine for all of Western Europe.

Twelve nations—Belgium, Denmark, France, Greece, Italy, the Netherlands, Norway, Sweden, Switzerland, the United Kingdom, West Germany, and Yugoslavia—signed the original CERN agreement on July 1, 1953. Yugoslavia withdrew from CERN in 1961, Austria joined in 1959, and Spain joined in 1961, withdrew in 1969, and rejoined in 1984. CERN's charter specified that all research carried on under its auspices would be made generally available to the scientific community and that it would engage in no military research.[13]

CERN's first accelerator, a 600-MeV synchrocyclotron (SC), was put into operation on August 1, 1957. Since that time three larger machines have been completed and put into operation. The most recent development at CERN is the Large Electron-Positron (LEP) collider which is expected to begin operation in 1990. LEP accelerates electron and positron beams in a tunnel 27 kilometers (17 miles) in circumference to energies of 50 GeV.

CERN has become one of the world's largest and most active research centers in physics. Its annual budget provides a glimpse of the scope of accelerator research today. Some twelve hundred scientists and engineers and an additional twenty-three hundred staff and support personnnel work at the center. In addition, some thirty-two hundred physicists from two hundred research

The broken white line shows the location of the synchrotron at CERN in Geneva, Switzerland.

centers in CERN member states, the United States, the Soviet Union, and Japan use CERN's facilities for all or part of their research.

The annual budget of about 680 million Swiss francs (about $450 million in 1987) is paid on a proportional basis by member nations. In 1985, West Germany contributed 24.7 percent of the total; France, 20.6 percent; Great Britain, 16.1 percent; and Italy, 13.3 percent; with the remaining 25.3 percent divided among the other nine member-nations.

CERN has had an illustrious record of accomplishments in its four-decade history. As early as 1959, CERN's proton synchrotron (PS) produced the first direct evidence of the decay of a pion to an electron and an antineutrino. Four years later, the same machine yielded the earliest photographs of interactions involving those tiny, peculiar, and elusive particles known as neutrinos.

Some of CERN's most exciting work has had to do with the search for rare particles known as W and Z bosons. These particles are vital keys to currently popular theories in particle physics. The earliest evidence for the particles came from PS experiments completed in 1973. And final confirmation of the particles themselves was obtained in 1983 by way of proton-antiproton collisions in the CERN's super proton synchrotron (SPS). This latest discovery earned the 1984 Nobel Prize in Physics for two leaders of the CERN SPS research, Carlo Rubbia and Simon van der Meer.

CERN is probably best known for its dramatic research at the forefront of particle physics. But, as at other accelerator centers, research and development on more practical problems goes on constantly. For example, the

*This computerized control room controls the
whole of CERN's complex of particle accelerators,
including the proton synchrotron (PS) and
the super proton synchrotron (SPS).*

SC can be used as a fixed-target accelerator using low-energy (about 600 MeV) beams to produce radioactive materials. These isotopes are used in diagnosis and treatment of disease, for various industrial applications, and in scientific research.

In fact, the work going on at CERN is a good illustration of the diverse ways in which particle accelerators today are used both for research and for many practical applications.

CHAPTER
FOUR

THE WORK OF
PARTICLE
ACCELERATORS

The earliest particle accelerators were sometimes called atom smashers. That name can be misleading for at least two reasons. First, the idea of "smashing" an atom suggests a kind of brute-force approach to research. But the work of particle accelerators is actually quite sophisticated and delicate. Accelerators are finely tuned instruments for improving our understanding of the structure of matter. In some ways, a particle accelerator is more like a high-powered microscope than a cannon.

Second, particle accelerators do more than analyze existing forms of matter. They actually create new subatomic particles. These particles do not exist here on earth under normal circumstances, although they conceivably may exist elsewhere in the universe under different circumstances. By studying these new particles, physicists are gaining a better understanding of the structure of matter, the nature of fundamental particles, and the forces that act among them.

Accelerators have uses beyond fundamental research also. They have been found to have many practical applications in fields such as medicine, technology, and industry.

The structure of the nucleus • What is matter made of? That question has intrigued scientists for centuries. The usual starting point in answering the question has been to assume that appearances are deceiving. That is, matter appears to be terribly complex because it exists in so many different forms. Just look at the variety of matter around you at this moment.

Yet, scientists have long believed that if you could break all forms of matter down into the smallest particles of which it is made, you would find a much simpler picture. For example, John Dalton, the eighteenth century English chemist, suggested that all matter consists of tiny, indivisible particles which he called atoms. In Dalton's view, an atom looked something like a very small marble, a grain of sand, or a ball bearing.

Nearly two centuries after Dalton, we still believe that atoms exist. But we know that they are not solid and indivisible. A century of research has shown that an atom has an internal structure, consisting on the first level of a nucleus and orbiting electrons.

But neither is the nucleus solid and indivisible, as had once been suspected. Instead, it too has structure that includes, at the very least, protons and neutrons. But how does one probe an object as small as a nucleus?

To answer that question we need to review some

basic ideas about the nature of light. Light is a wave, somewhat similar to a water wave. The distance between crests of the wave is known as the wavelength. The wavelength of visible light is very small, about 10^{-7} meter (10^{-5} inch). In contrast, the wavelength of a water wave is about a meter (a yard) or more.

We see an object when light waves reflect off that object to our eyes. Reflection occurs when the wavelength of the light is smaller than the size of the object. If the object is smaller than the wavelength of the light, it will not be visible with ordinary light. For such objects, we can use forms of radiation with shorter wavelengths. An electron microscope, for example, shines a beam of electrons on objects. The wavelength of the electron beam is about 10^{-10} meter (about 10^{-8} inch), a thousand times smaller than that of visible light. Objects too small to be seen with a light microscope may be visible in an electron microscope.

Atomic nuclei are no more than 10^{-15} meter (10^{-13} inch) across, much too small to be seen even with an electron microscope. Something with an even shorter wavelength is needed to see into a nucleus. One solution to that problem is to use rapidly moving particles, which also travel as waves. The wavelength of such a particle is inversely proportional to its velocity. The faster the particle moves, the smaller its wavelength.

Particles from a particle accelerator move at nearly the speed of light and have wavelengths of about 10^{-16} meter (about 10^{-14} inch). With this improved "microscope," scientists have been able to probe into the structure of the nucleus itself. They have learned that even protons and neutrons are themselves compound particles, consisting of smaller units called quarks.

Particle accelerators can thus be imagined as an extension of light and electron microscopes. The rapidly moving, high-energy particles they produce have very small wavelengths, allowing us a better and better look at the internal structure of nuclei.

Creating new particles • Perhaps the most exciting goal of accelerator research is the creation of entirely new particles. That goal is possible because of a discovery made by Albert Einstein in 1905. At one time scientists had considered mass (the "stuff" of which all things are made) and energy (the driving force that makes things happen) to be two entirely different phenomena. Einstein was able to show that they are not really distinct but are closely interrelated. He showed that energy can actually exist in the form of matter and that the annihilation of matter can result in the formation of energy.

For example, suppose two light beams (forms of energy) are directed at each other. Under the proper conditions, the collision of these light beams can result in the formation of a pair of electrons. The energy of the light beams is transformed into the mass of the electrons. Similarly, the collision of two electrons can result in the opposite effect. The electrons disappear and are replaced by a burst of energy in the form of light.

Einstein expressed the relationship between energy and mass in a now familiar formula, $E = mc^2$, where E stands for energy, m for mass, and c for the speed of light. This explains why physicists often use energy terms to talk about the mass of a particle. For example, the mass of a proton is said to be 938 MeV, and that of an electron, 0.511 MeV.

The energy-mass relationship has great significance for particle accelerators. It suggests that energy produced in accelerators can be converted to mass, that is, can be used to create particles. Furthermore, since the amount of energy produced in accelerators is much greater than what we normally encounter in nature, we might expect accelerators to be able to generate particles unlike those with which we are already familiar.

Imagine two beams of electrons that collide with each other within an accelerator. That collision will involve enormous amounts of energy. Some of that energy may appear in the form of new particles. The amount of energy carried by the colliding particles determines the mass those newly created particles can have and thus the particles formed. For example, a particle known as the neutral pion can form if two colliding particles have available more than 135 MeV of energy. A machine that gives its particles less than this amount of energy would never be able to "find" (that is, create) a neutral pion.

Perhaps you can see, then, what happens when larger and larger accelerators are built. The maximum energy available with each new accelerator increases. That means that particles that could not be produced with smaller, less energetic machines can now be produced. And that has been the pattern in particle physics over the past half century. Every time a new accelerator was turned on or its energy turned up, one or more new particles were capable of being discovered.

By 1960, particle accelerators had yielded more than a hundred new subatomic particles. Most of these particles were extremely unstable, decaying less than a billionth of a second to two or more other particles. Physicists had begun to refer, only half-jokingly, to their "zoo" of subatomic particles.

The particle zoo presented physicists with a dilemma. On the one hand, each new particle discovery was cause for excitement and celebration. Physicists scrambled to explain where the particle came from, what its significance was, and how it fit with dozens of other basic particles also being discovered about the same time. Puzzles such as these are exactly the spark that fires so many scientific researchers. So these were wonderful times for particle physicists. On the other hand, physicists had begun to wonder where they were going in their study of matter. After all, one goal of their search was to find the fundamentals of nature. And scientists firmly believe that in nature "fundamental" means "simple." It seemed most unlikely that nature consisted of a hundred (or even a few dozen) basic particles. So scientists in the 1960s could have been excused for dreaming wistfully of the recent past when the fundamental particles of matter could be counted on one hand.

The standard model • Yet another goal of accelerator research, then, was to sort out the truly fundamental particles of nature, find out what their properties were, and study the forces that acted between them. By the mid-1960s, theoretical physicists had begun to find a way in which the flood of new particles could be classified and explained. Theoretical physicists spend most of their time developing the major ideas of physics in mathematical terms. In contrast, experimental physicists test those ideas in a laboratory and produce the factual basis for the next round of theories.

That system of classification and explanation is known as the Standard Model. The Standard Model attempts to describe the truly fundamental particles of matter and the forces that exist among those fundamental particles.

The key to unraveling the particle zoo puzzle was the assumption that only a handful of the known particles are really fundamental. By fundamental we mean that a particle appears to be indivisible. It does not consist of smaller particles and cannot be broken down into anything simpler. Two groups of particles, named leptons and quarks, belong in this category (Table 2). Both leptons and quarks are grouped in three levels (also called families or generations), depending on the energy required to produce them.

Six leptons exist: the electron and electron neutrino, the muon and muon neutrino, and the tau and tau

Table 2. The Fundamental Particles

Level	Quarks		Leptons		Energy Level
3	top (truth)	t	tau	τ	origin of the universe most powerful particle accelerators
	bottom (beauty)	b	tau neutrino	ν_τ	
2	strange	s	muon	μ	cosmic ray events most particle accelerators
	charm	c	muon neutrino	ν_μ	
1	up	u	electron	ϵ	everyday objects and events
	down	d	electron neutrino	ν_ϵ	

neutrino. Leptons in level 1, the electron and electron neutrino, are present all around us in everyday objects and phenomena. Although you can't see them, electrons are a part of everything you deal with in your life. Indeed, you can collect some electrons simply by rubbing your feet on a carpet on a dry day. When you touch a metal doorknob, the tiny spark you feel and hear is the collected electrons jumping from your finger to the metal. Electron neutrinos are also abundant in everyday life. They are much more difficult to observe, however. Since they pass through matter without interacting, highly specialized methods are necessary to detect them.

Leptons in levels 2 and 3 are much less common. They form only when very large amounts of energy are available. The muon, for example, has been known for a long time, but primarily as a product of cosmic ray showers in our atmosphere. Cosmic rays are powerful forms of energy that originate in outer space and bombard our atmosphere continuously. They are one of the most energetic forms of radiation known to humans. When they strike atoms in the earth's outer atmosphere, they produce reactions similar to those that take place in powerful accelerators. Conditions such as these are necessary for the production of the level-2 leptons.

Level-3 leptons represent a still higher energy level. This amount of energy can no longer be found in the natural world, although it was present at the creation of the universe (the "Big Bang"). The world's most powerful accelerators are able to attain the lower limit of this level, and the SSC will reach even higher into this range.

The other truly fundamental particles—six types of quarks—were nothing other than an abstract idea when first proposed in the 1960s. No one had seen even the first-level quarks at that time even though they, like the electron and electron neutrino, exist all around us. In fact, quarks have still not been observed as free particles outside the confines of protons, neutrons, or other complex particles.

Particle physicists have shown a sense of humor in naming quarks. They have named those in the first level, for example, as "up" and "down," those in the second level as "strange" and "charm," and those in the third level as either "top" and "bottom" or "truth" and "beauty." When later research showed that each kind of quark can exist in a variety of forms, a little like positive and negative electric charge, the forms were given the names of colors. Thus, an up quark can exist as a "red" up quark, a "yellow" up quark, or a "blue" up quark. Terms such as "up," "down," "truth," "beauty," "yellow," and "blue" have no connection whatsoever with the same qualities we know of in everyday life.

The problem for experimental physicists was to prove that quarks really do exist and are not just some pleasant, helpful, but imaginary concept. To do so, they needed powerful particle accelerators that could probe the internal structure of protons and neutrons. The first experiments of this kind were conducted at SLAC in 1969. Powerful electron beams from the linac were directed at protons and neutrons. The wavelength of those beams was small enough to look inside the proton and the neutron. The beams reflected in such a way as to indicate the presence of tiny particles *within* the proton and *within* the neutron. The three tiny particles found there corresponded in every way to the quarks predicted by theoretical physicists. The first concrete evidence for quarks (the up and down varieties, in this case) was in.

Physicists were intrigued by these results. Sixty-six years earlier, Rutherford had discovered that atoms consist of smaller particles (nuclei and electrons). The SLAC experiment showed that protons and neutrons consist of even smaller particles (quarks). The obvious next question is whether quarks also consist of even smaller particles yet. Right now, physicists disagree about the answer to this question and are probably about evenly split as to whether the answer is yes or no. Since no existing or planned accelerator is big enough to answer the question, the debate about quarks as fundamental particles may go on for some time.

We now believe that most particles in the zoo consist of various combinations of quarks. For example, a proton consists of two up quarks and one down quark. We can represent this arrangement as: uud. Similarly, a neutron consists of one up quark and two down quarks, or udd. The particle named sigma zero consists of one up, one down, and one strange quark (uds). Particles such as the proton, neutron, and sigma that consist of two or three quarks bound to each other are known as hadrons. Most particles in the zoo are hadrons.

The forces between particles • The Standard Model describes not only the fundamental particles of nature, but also the forces that act between particles. Learning more about these forces is another objective of accelerator research. Scientists currently recognize four fundamental forces in nature. These are the gravitational, electromagnetic, strong, and weak forces (Table 3). You are prob-

Table 3. The Fundamental Forces

Type	Relative Strength	Acts On	Effective Distance	Mediating Particle(s)
Gravitational	10^{-39}	all particles	very long	graviton (?)
Weak	10^{-5}	leptons, quarks	very short	W^+, W^-, Z^0 bosons
Electromagnetic	10^{-2}	charged particles	very long	photon
Strong	1	quarks	very short	gluon

ably familiar with the first two of these forces. The gravitational force acts between any two objects in the universe, no matter how close together or how far apart they are. The electromagnetic force acts on all charged particles, also at any distance.

You may not know as much about the weak and strong forces. Both act over very short distances, much smaller than the diameter of an atom. The strong force is aptly named. It's 10^{39} (that's a 1 followed by thirty-nine 0's) times stronger than the gravitational force and a hundred times stronger than the electromagnetic force you experience every day. The strong force is powerful enough to hold protons together in the nucleus even though we expect them to repel each other because of their like electrical charge. The strong force also holds quarks together to make other particles in the zoo. The two up and one down quarks that make up a proton, for example, are held together by a strong force.

At ordinary energies, the weak force is a hundred thousandth as strong as the strong force and a thousand times weaker than the electromagnetic force. It is responsible for certain kinds of radioactive decay that take place within nuclei.

Physicists believe that the four basic forces act between particles by means of other particles called mediating or gauge particles. This belief is based on the mass-energy relationship described earlier. Just as mass can be described in terms of an energy equivalent, so an energy relationship can be expressed in terms of a particle.

For example, an electromagnetic force of repulsion between two protons tends to push the particles away from each other. Physicists say that the electromagnetic force is "carried" between the two protons by means of the photon, the mediating particle for the electromagnetic force. Light, X rays, infrared and ultraviolet radiation, radio waves, and microwaves are all forms of electromagnetic radiation that are also mediated by the photon.

Similarly, the strong force that holds quarks together within a proton or a neutron is thought to be mediated by a particle with the very suggestive name of gluon because it's the "glue" that holds quarks together. No one has yet found a free gluon, but indirect evidence to support its existence has been accumulating for a number of years. In 1980, researchers at SLAC reported what they thought might be a two-gluon particle, which they called gluonium or a glueball.[14] In any case, most particle physicists are now convinced by indirect evidence that gluons do exist.

One of the great achievements in particle physics in recent years was the discovery of the mediating particles for the weak force. The Standard model had predicted the existence of three particles, the W^+, W^-, and Z^0

bosons, as carriers of the weak force. Research conducted at CERN in the late 1970s and early 1980s finally provided solid evidence for the existence of these particles. Only the graviton remains a completely theoretical particle with no experimental evidence for its existence.

By the late 1980s, physicists stood at yet another threshold. The Standard Model had—at least for the moment—solved many troubling questions about the fundamental nature of matter. The members of the particle zoo had begun to fall into place. The relationship among the four fundamental forces and between forces and particles was beginning to make more sense.

But some basic questions remained unanswered. And the very success of the Standard Model had raised even more puzzles for physicists. The stage was set for the next step in particle accelerator development: the Superconducting Super Collider.

Particle accelerators and applied research • Particle accelerators are probably best known for their role in basic research. Basic research is conducted for the purpose of discovering new facts about the natural world. Those facts may lead eventually to some practical benefit: improved health or better technology, for example. But the possible benefits are not the reason for doing basic research in the first place. Such research is designed and carried out primarily to satisfy some scientist's curiosity about the way nature works.

Applied research, on the other hand, aims to solve a specific, practical problem. The development of new medicines and better communication systems are examples of applied research.

Accelerating particles to high speeds in order to blow atomic nuclei apart and see what's inside, to make new particles, and to study the forces of nature is an example of basic research. When people ask what the point of such research is, what good it will do, scientists can only say, "We don't know. We are trying to find out more about the structure of matter. Who can say what good (if any) that knowledge will ever do?" As the English physicist Michael Faraday once said, when asked about practical applications for the principle of electromagnetic induction which he had discovered, "What use is a newborn babe?"

On the other hand, not all the work done with accelerators is basic research. Some is applied research with the aim of solving practical technological problems. Among these practical jobs is the manufacture of radioactive isotopes, the diagnosis and treatment of disease, and the solution of industrial and technical problems.

Particle accelerators as "X-ray" machines

Electrons accelerated in a linac leave the machine with a great deal of energy. They are in some ways similar to X rays. That's hardly surprising since X-ray machines themselves are a kind of small particle accelerator. Therefore, electrons from a linac can be used in some of the ways X rays have been used.

A typical example is the "X-raying" of metal welds with a linac electron beam. Finding out whether a weld has been done correctly, without destroying the material containing the weld, can be a difficult task. By using a linac electron beam, one can "X-ray" the metal to evaluate the weld or to look for cracks in the metal itself. Linac electron beams can be used in a similar way to look for cancers or other tumors. "X-ray" photos taken this way can tell a physician the size, shape, and location of diseased tissue.

Accelerators in medical therapy

In addition to their use in diagnosis (discovering disease), particle accelerators can be used in therapy (curing disease). One example is the Midwest Institute for Neutron Therapy (MINT) at Fermilab. Protons from the Fermi linac collide with a beryllium metal target producing neutrons. These neutrons are then used to irradiate cancerous tumors. The treatment has turned out to be especially useful with tumors of the salivary glands, bladder, and prostate, as well as with other forms of cancer that cannot be treated with surgery.

Accelerators as sources of radioactive materials

Accelerators are also used widely to produce radioactive materials. At one time, scientists had to depend completely on natural sources for the radioactive materials they needed for industrial, medical, or research use. Then they learned how to convert stable, nonradioactive substances into radioactive forms.

The trick is to bombard ordinary, stable atoms with high-speed protons, electrons, and other subatomic particles. When the particle-bullets strike an ordinary, stable atom, changes take place in its nucleus. A proton, neutron, or some combination of these may be knocked out of the nucleus, changing the atom into something different from what is was before. When the target nucleus and particle-bullet are properly chosen, a new radioactive atom is formed.

Radioactive materials are in great demand today. They are widely used in medical diagnosis and treatment, in many industrial processes, and in scientific research. Some smaller particle accelerators are now used exclusively for the manufacture of these much-needed radioactive materials.

The all-purpose cyclotron

Illustrative of the many-faceted capability of the modern cyclotron is the machine now in use at the University of California at Davis. This machine is a labor of love by Dr. Thomas A. Cahill, director of the university's Crocker Nuclear Laboratory, and his students. In the tradition of the first Lawrence cyclotron, the Davis machine was built and is being operated on a shoestring. In fact, its magnet was salvaged from an earlier Lawrence cyclotron originally put together in 1939.

One use to which the Davis cyclotron is being put is in the analysis of old documents. Slow proton beams from the cyclotron are used to bombard old letters, maps, and other documents producing X rays having certain wavelengths. Each chemical element has its own characteristic wavelength. Therefore, when protons strike atoms in the ink, paint, and paper in these documents, the X rays they produce enable scientists to determine the composition of materials in the document. From this, an estimate of the document's probable age can often be made.

Dr. Cahill's team is finding dozens of other uses for the cyclotron also, including the study of solar radiation, analysis of air over Los Angeles, measurement of acid rain, and determination of air quality in certain national parks. The machine also produces radioactive materials for diagnosis and treatment of cancer.[15]

The uses of
synchrotron radiation

And finally, even one of the negative features of accelerators has been put to use. Synchrotron radiation, once a bane of electron synchrotrons, is now a valuable tool in research and technology. Synchrotron radiation has many of the characteristics of X rays, but it excels X rays in some important ways.

For example, synchrotron radiation is more intense—sometimes a thousand times more intense—than X rays.[16] That property is utilized in the manufacture of integrated circuits for use in computing services. Normally the pattern for an integrated circuit is etched into a material using a beam of X rays. The X rays cut into the material, forming the pattern needed for the circuit on its surface. The etching process must be completed quickly, however, typically in a second or so. The greater intensity of synchrotron radiation makes it a better tool for this kind of etching than are normal X rays.

Synchrotron radiation also travels in a narrow, sharply

defined beam like that of a laser beam. This property makes it possible to form very sharp, highly defined lines in the integrated circuit.

Synchrotron radiation also differs from X rays in that it is pulsed. Remember that electrons in a synchrotron travel not in a continuous beam but in bunches. Each time a bunch of electrons are accelerated in a synchrotron, they emit a pulse of synchrotron radiation. These pulses may occur anywhere from a hundred thousand to five hundred million times per second.

Researchers can make use of the pulsed character of synchrotron radiation. For example, a chemist may want to study the changes that take place during a chemical reaction. Many chemical reactions normally occur very rapidly and are completed in less than a second. Researchers can focus pulsed synchrotron radiation on such a reaction and "take a new picture" of the reaction during each pulse. Putting together these pictures gives the researcher an overview of the events that took place, rapidly, during the reaction.

Yet a third property of synchrotron radiation is the range of wavelengths on which it is carried. The wavelength of X-rays normally ranges from about 10^{-8} meter (10^{-6} inch; "soft" X rays) to about 10^{-12} meter (10^{-10} inch; "hard" X rays). The wavelength of synchrotron radiation, on the other hand, typically extends from about 10^{-5} meter (10^{-3} inch) to about 10^{-11} meter (10^{-9} inch). One way in which this property is used is in the process of angiography, the "X-raying" of arteries. A liquid containing the element iodine is injected into a person's bloodstream. A synchrotron radiation beam is then focused on the person's body. The beam is split into two parts, one with a wavelength that is absorbed by iodine, the other with a wavelength that is not absorbed by the element. The two beams pass through the person's body and then into detectors. Comparing the image produced by the two beams gives a picture of blood vessels in the person's body showing any damage that may be present.

Synchrotron radiation has come a long way since its earliest years as a "trouble-maker" for accelerator designers. Today, synchrotron radiation has become a powerful research tool and technological aid. Machines are built and operated for the purpose of producing synchrotron radiation. By 1988, electron synchrotrons were operated at least partially or completely as sources for synchrotron radiation for more than five thousand researchers throughout the world.[17]

CHAPTER FIVE

A PROGRAM FOR THE SSC

Particle physics has reached a crossroads. As has happened so often in the past, existing accelerators have been pushed to their limits. Physicists no longer expect major breakthroughs from the Tevatron, SLAC, DESY, CERN, and other giant machines. Further progress at the forefront of particle physics will come only if and when a new and larger accelerator—the Superconducting Super Collider, for example—is built. As one scientist has said, "Scientifically, the supercollider is mandatory. We're at the same place that we were at the turn of the century. We have a standard model that explains almost everything. But there are just a few little nagging details . . . that we know don't fit."[18]

What do physicists expect to learn by using the SSC? In some ways, the most honest answer to that question might be that if physicists knew what they were going to find, they wouldn't have to build the machine at all. As two physicists have said about the SSC: "We must acknowledge history's lesson [in working with new accelerators] that surprises have been our most frequent lot."[19]

This comment reflects a critical point about the SSC. It will be a machine that can do things no machine has ever been able to do. We simply can't say what new and surprising discoveries might come from its use. The fact is, however, that physicists do have some fairly specific expectations from their research with the SSC. These expectations arise out of previous successes in theoretical and experimental particle physics. The Standard Model has worked well in explaining discoveries already made with particle accelerators and provides predictions for new events that might be looked for at higher energies.

For example, we think we understand the nature of quarks, leptons, and hadrons reasonably well. Also we seem to have a reasonably satisfactory knowledge of the strong, weak, and electromagnetic forces. But some important questions in particle physics remain. These include problems such as the structure of quarks and leptons, the unification of the fundamental forces, remaining difficulties with the four fundamental forces, and the question of the origin of mass and its relation to charge.

The structure of quarks and leptons • One goal of SSC research is to find out whether quarks and leptons are truly fundamental particles. For the present, the Standard Model assumes they are. But the recurring theme in particle physics has been that seemingly "elementary" particles turn out to consist of yet smaller units.

First, atoms were shown to be made of protons,

neutrons, and electrons. Then protons and neutrons were found to consist of quarks. Maybe quarks and leptons are themselves compound particles whose smaller components have yet to be discovered. Physicists have some reason to think that this may be so. For example, the relationship between quarks and leptons shows an interesting pattern. Each family consists of three parallel pairs of particles that exist at certain energy levels. You can look back at Table 2 in Chapter Four to review this relationship. Further, the particles at each level have greater masses than the particles below them. Some physicists think that these patterns may mean that quarks and leptons are both made of even smaller particles yet.

The unification of forces • Another goal of SSC research has to do with the relationship among the four fundamental forces. Most physicists now believe that these forces are not really distinct but are associated with one another in some fundamental sense. Finding a way to show how these forces are related—developing a unified theory of forces—has been a goal of physicists, including Albert Einstein, for at least half a century.

The assumption has been that our view of forces is somewhat limited by the energy levels with which we are most familiar. In the everyday world, where events take place at a few keV, electromagnetism, gravity, the strong force, and the weak force *are* distinct. For example, the weak force operates over a range of only about 10^{-17} meter (10^{-15} inch) while the electromagnetic force acts over an infinite distance. Physicists believe that such differences do not exist at very high energy levels (from 100 GeV to 15 TeV). They think that in the upper part of this range not four forces, but only one, exists.

Since the 1950s physicists have been working on theories that show how the four forces might be related to each other. The most successful of those theories have been those that try to relate the electromagnetic and weak forces to each other. According to those theories, the differences between the electromagnetic force and the weak force do not exist at energy levels greater than about 100 GeV. Above that point, the theories say, we should be able to find a single force, the electroweak force.

Theories like that of the electroweak force are useful only if they can be tested experimentally. A theory has to suggest one or more specific experiments in which researchers can look for a particular event. If that event occurs, the theory is at least partially confirmed. The more often predicted events occur, the more confidence we have in the theory that predicted them. Sometimes a single prediction is critical. Finding evidence for that single prediction is likely to convince scientists that the theory is probably correct.

In the case of the electroweak theory, the critical prediction was that of the W and Z bosons. Prior to 1983, no mediating particle for the weak force had yet been found. That missing information left an important gap in the Standard Model. The electroweak theory predicted the existence of not one, but three, mediating particles. It also predicted what the characteristics of those particles would be. It said that one of the particles would be positively charged (the W^+ boson), one would be negatively charged (the W^- boson), and one would be electrically neutral (the Z^0 boson), all with rest masses of about 100 GeV.

Experiments conducted at CERN in 1983 found all

three bosons, with just the properties predicted for them. The match between prediction and experiment was so good that physicists regarded the electroweak theory as essentially confirmed.[20]

The next step toward the goal of unification would be to demonstrate the relationship between the electroweak and strong forces. Direct evidence for an electroweak-strong unification would probably require energies approximating a trillion TeV. Such energies are beyond the wildest dreams of the SSC designers, beyond the dreams of science fiction writers, in fact.

Still, some evidence for this unification might show up at lower energies. Unification theories often hypothesize the existence of a particle (or class of particles) known as the Higgs boson. This particle was first proposed by Professor Peter W. Higgs at the University of Edinburgh. The Higgs boson began as a purely mathematical concept introduced to make the Standard Model more internally consistent mathematically. No one can yet say whether the Higgs boson actually exists, although physicists believe that something like it must exist.[21] In any case, the Higgs boson has proved to be useful in making predictions of events that might be expected in the range of 1 to 20 TeV and higher. The discovery of a Higgs boson might, therefore, provide another step forward in the development of unification theories.

Problems with the electroweak theory • The fact that the electroweak theory has been confirmed and that it seems to work well does not mean that no problems remain. For example, in its earliest forms the electroweak theory was able to make good predictions up to a certain point, but no further. Physicists would like the theory to be able to make predictions for all situations to any degree of precision. Also, some of the predictions made by the theory were nonsensical. In one case, for example, the theory predicted the probability of a certain event's happening to be more than 100 percent. That prediction was equivalent to saying that the event was more than certain to occur. Such a prediction is obviously absurd.

Once again, the Higgs boson comes to the rescue. Purely as a mathematical device, it shows how the electroweak theory can be extended to a wider variety of situations with a higher degree of precision. Further, the presence of the Higgs boson may eliminate some of the more absurd theoretical predictions, such as that of greater-than-100 percent probabilities. The discovery of a Higgs boson would, therefore, make the electroweak theory an even more powerful predictive tool.

The origin of mass • Confirmation of the electroweak theory in 1983 raised an intriguing problem. Under normal conditions, the mass of the mediating particle for the electromagnetic force, the photon, is zero and the masses of the mediating particles for the weak force, the W^+, W^-, and Z^0 bosons, are respectively 82 GeV, 82 GeV, and 93 GeV. Yet experiments show that at energies greater than 100 GeV, the mass of all four mediating particles is effectively zero. The question, then, is what happens when the two forces become distinct from each other at energy levels below 100 GeV to give the W and Z bosons their mass? Where does their mass come from?

This question is a crucial one for scientists. Most of us take for granted the fact that particles have mass.

Nonscientists may know, for example, that a proton weighs something, but they usually don't wonder how the proton got its mass in the first place. But scientists *would* like to know how particles get their mass. If they can answer that question for W and Z bosons, they may be able to generalize the answer to other particles.

Once again, the Higgs boson may provide a solution to this problem. The Higgs boson is a mediating particle for a force field, the Higgs field. A particle passing through the Higgs field picks up energy from the field. Since energy is equivalent to mass, the interaction of the particle with the field gives mass to the particle. One writer compares the gain of mass by a particle as it passes through the Higgs field to the way blotting paper soaks up water. He says that the particle " 'eat[s]' the Higgs boson to gain weight." [22]

You can probably see why physicists hold out great hopes for the Higgs field and the Higgs boson. The Higgs theory certainly has the potential for solving many existing difficulties in particle physics. Yet, many questions about the theory are troublesome. Perhaps most basic is the way in which the theory was developed. As one particle physicist has said, "Existing methods for dealing with these questions involve the introduction of many unexplained numerical constants into the theory, a situation that many physicists find arbitrary and thus unsatisfying." [23]

The theory also presents difficulties, since the necessary tests are not always clear. For example, there appears to be no constraint on the mass of the Higgs boson. It might range anywhere from a few GeV to more than 1 TeV. [24] Existing accelerators could search the lower part of this range for the particle, but only the SSC will be powerful enough to search the upper part. The SSC has a crucial role, therefore, in clarifying the whole concept of the Higgs theory and determining whether it is anything other than a clever, but unreal, representation of the nature of matter.

A shopping list of questions for the SSC • Particle physicists can list dozens of similar, specific questions they hope the SSC will answer.[25] For example, what is the nature of the "dark matter" that makes up so much of our universe? Scientists now know that up to 90 percent of the matter in our universe is invisible.[26] We detect its presence only in phenomena such as the effect it has on the distribution and motion of galaxies and the expansion of the universe. Is it possible that neutrinos have a very small mass that would account for this "dark matter"?

Also, why don't we find more antimatter (positrons, antiprotons, and antineutrons) than we do? At the creation of the universe, the chances of creating matter and antimatter were probably about equal. Yet when we survey the universe today, we find much more matter than antimatter. Was antimatter destroyed in the very early moments of creation? If so, how? Are there regions of the universe today in which antimatter predominates over matter? How *do* we explain the preponderance of matter over antimatter in that part of the universe we can study?

And the questions go on: Do quarks exist only within hadrons, or is it possible for them to exist in a free, unbound state? Why do interactions involving the weak force violate a conservation law (known as mirror symmetry) that holds true for all other known reactions? What is the nature and origin of electric charge? Do yet other kinds of forces and/or particles exist that we have not yet found? What is the relationship between the gravitational force and the electroweak and strong forces? If the Higgs boson does exist, is it as a single particle or is there a group of related Higgs bosons? Is the Higgs boson an elementary or composite particle?

The smallest and the oldest • Finally, physicists anticipate that the SSC will act as a time machine, taking them back to the earliest moments of the universe's birth. At present, scientists believe that the universe was created in a single "big bang" about fifteen billion years ago. At the instant the Big Bang occurred, only energy existed. At the first moment after the Big Bang, energy began to change form and appear as matter. These changes took place at unimaginably high temperatures and in unimaginably short periods of time.

According to current theories (Figure 9), only 10^{-43} second after the Big Bang, 10^{15} TeV of energy was packed into a volume smaller than the head of a pin. Prior to this instant, only a single force existed in the universe. That force corresponds to the unified force which physicists are trying to understand and describe today. We can't say very much about that force yet except to describe it as the primordial force from which the four forces we know today—gravitation, the strong force, the weak force, and electromagnetism—emerged.

At 10^{-43} second, the first distinct type of force, gravitation, emerged. Had any physicists been present at that moment, they would have been able to distinguish between the two forces: gravitation and a strong/elec-

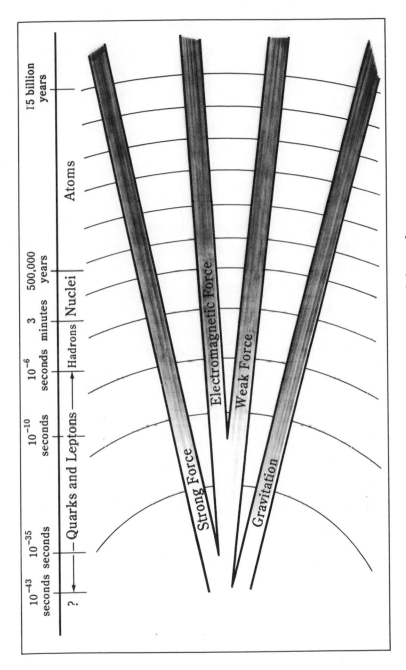

Figure 9. Early history of the universe

troweak force. At 10^{-34} second and 10^{12} TeV, the strong force broke from the electroweak force. Our imaginary physicists would then have been able to distinguish three forces: gravitation, the strong force, and the electroweak force. At 10^{-10} second and 100 GeV, the electromagnetic and weak forces parted company, and the world with which we are familiar, containing four distinct forces, came into being. Finally, at about a microsecond, quarks combined to make protons and neutrons and, a minute later, atoms began to form. At this point, the universe as we know it today—four forces and quarks and leptons tied up in atoms—had taken form.[27]

Much of this story is speculation, of course, since no one actually observed the Big Bang. However, particle accelerators such as the SSC now provide a way of "looking back" and checking on this theory. As we build accelerators with higher and higher energies, we can create environments more and more like the early universe, when energy levels were in the GeV–TeV range, rather than in the keV range we see today.

One might compare this use of accelerators to the showing of a movie about the history of the universe, only in reverse. The movie starts at "the end"—that is, with our world as we know it today—and goes backward in time. All we have to start with ("the end") is a low-energy world where events take place in the keV energy range. As we build accelerators of higher energies, though, we can see earlier parts of the movie when the universe contained much more energy, in the MeV, GeV, and TeV range. Eventually, with the most powerful accelerators we can build, we approach the beginning of the movie, the origin of the universe. At these high energies we see, in reverse, the separation of the four forces from one primordial force and the formation of quarks and leptons.

By creating energies in the range of 100 GeV, accelerators have already re-created conditions at the 10^{-10} second A.B.B. (After Big Bang) time. In the CERN experiments leading to the discovery of the W and Z bosons, the early history of the universe was reversed, large amounts of energy were created, and the electroweak symmetry was reestablished.

To complete our backward-running movie, we would have to go all the way back to 10^{-34} or 10^{-43} second A.B.B. when energies reached 10^{12}–10^{15} TeV. At those energies, we might be able to see the electroweak force merge with the strong force and later the strong/electroweak force merge with gravitation. And we might see all matter change back to its original form, energy.

But humans are not likely to find a way of building a machine that can produce that much energy. So we probably won't be able to run the movie all the way back to its very beginning. Nonetheless, with each increase in accelerator energy, we are able to turn back the story of the universe's history by one more frame. All of which adds an intriguing footnote to the story of the SSC. With the construction of this machine, scientists move closer to tying together their studies of the smallest objects in the universe—the core of the atomic nucleus—with the biggest question of all: the origin of the universe itself.

CHAPTER SIX

DESIGN OF THE SSC

To many Americans, news of the proposed SSC may have sounded like an exciting breakthrough in technology. Exciting it certainly is, but hardly a breakthrough, for the SSC, like most inventions in science, combines ideas that have been tried out and, for the most part, are already in use elsewhere. In fact, all of the major components of the SSC were tested at Fermilab's Tevatron before the SSC was ever conceived. The SSC is less a "new" machine than one that contains the most up-to-date existing accelerator technology.

Perhaps the most impressive feature of the SSC is its sheer size (Figure 10). The main ring will have a circumference of 82.944 kilometers (51.539 miles). In comparison, the ring in the largest existing accelerator, the Tevatron at Fermilab, has a circumference of about 6.4 kilometers (4.0 miles).[28]

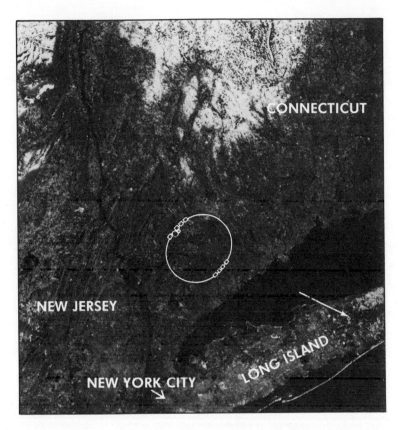

Figure 10. Schematic of the SSC overlaid on a satellite photograph of New York. Arrow points to the existing circular accelerator at Brookhaven.

Visitors to the SSC site will be largely unaware of the ring itself. It will be buried at least 6 meters (20 feet) underground to prevent the escape of any radiation that may result from experiments in the accelerator.

The ring itself consists of a concrete tunnel about 3 meters (10 feet) in diameter. It contains the heart of the

SSC—two metal tubes a few centimeters in diameter and 70 centimeters (28 inches) apart (Figure 11).

Protons will be accelerated to energies of 20 TeV within the tubes. One beam of protons will travel in one direction in the upper tube, while the other beam will travel in the opposite direction in the lower tube. Protons will travel in bunches of about ten billion in a cylindrical space about 0.2 millimeter (0.008 inch) wide and 15 centimeters (5.9 inches) long. The concrete tunnel will also contain the accelerator magnets, electrical equipment, and small cars on which workers and material can be transported.

The main ring described here is actually the fifth and final accelerator in the SSC. Protons begin their journey to the ring in a linear accelerator that provides them with an energy of 600 MeV. From the linac, the protons travel through three smaller synchrotrons that raise their energy first to 8 GeV, then from 8 GeV to 100 GeV, and finally from 100 GeV to 1 TeV. At that point, they enter the large, 83-kilometer ring and are accelerated to their maximum energy of 20 TeV.

The challenge of the magnets • The most difficult technical problem in designing the SSC involved the magnets. The magnets used in particle accelerators are not like bar or horseshoe magnets, with which you may be familiar. Instead, they are electromagnets, devices that use electric currents to generate magnetic fields. Electromagnets are much preferred to bar or horseshoe magnets because they can generate stronger magnetic fields.

Bending and focusing 20-TeV proton beams using traditional magnets would have been enormously expen-

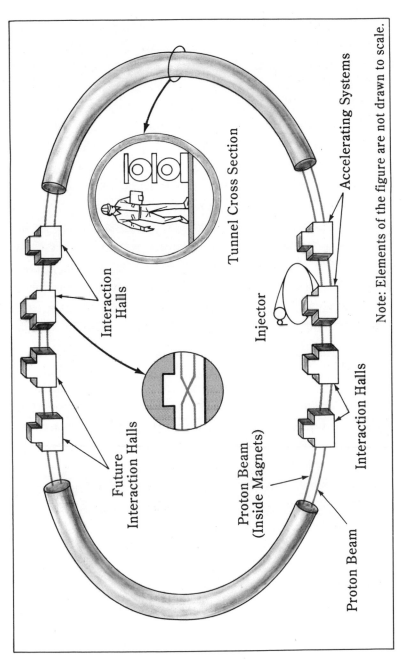

Interaction Halls

Future Interaction Halls

Tunnel Cross Section

Proton Beam (Inside Magnets)

Injector

Accelerating Systems

Interaction Halls

Proton Beam

Note: Elements of the figure are not drawn to scale.

Figure 11. Schematic of the SSC

sive and difficult. Designers estimate that traditional magnets in an SSC-type machine would have required 4 billion watts of power. That's more than the combined output of the three largest nuclear power plants in the United States in 1988. [29] Such an expense would have made the machine much too costly to operate.

Fortunately, an alternative solution has been known to scientists for some time: the use of superconducting magnets. Scientists have known since 1911 that some materials lose their resistance to electric current at very low temperatures. By "very low," we mean close to absolute zero, the lowest temperature possible, or $-273°C$ ($-459°F$). At such temperatures, the materials present no resistance to an electric current; they become superconducting. Once an electric current gets started in a superconducting material, the current travels essentially forever.

The first practical superconducting alloys were produced in about 1960 and put to use in bubble chambers soon thereafter. Experiences with superconducting magnets at Fermilab have demonstrated that they are just what is needed to make the SSC concept a reality. The cost of energy to operate superconducting magnets is only about 1 percent of the 4 billion watts needed for traditional magnets, well within a reasonable cost of operating the SSC. Also, the magnetic field produced by superconducting magnets is stronger than that from traditional magnets. If the SSC *could* have been built using traditional magnets, it would have had a circumference three times larger than that of the proposed SSC.

Superconducting magnets do pose a new problem

for accelerator designers, however. Arrangements must be made the keep the magnets at the very low temperatures needed to maintain superconductivity. This is accomplished by surrounding the magnets with liquid helium at a temperature of about $-269°C$ ($-452°F$). The cost of refrigerating the 2,000,000 liters (500,000 gallons) of liquid helium partially replaces the cost of energy loss in traditional magnets. That cost, about 30 million watts of power, is still less than the cost of power used in the largest existing accelerator today, however.[30]

After the original design of the SSC was completed, physicists received news of an exciting discovery. Researchers in superconductivity began finding new materials, in late 1986, which remained superconducting at temperatures much higher than those planned for the SSC. Materials that showed superconductivity above $-196°C$ ($-321°F$), for example, were reported in 1987. This news was particularly promising since $-196°C$ is the boiling point of nitrogen. Cooling the magnetic coils with liquid nitrogen rather than liquid helium would be a simpler, less expensive task. Some of the most optimistic scientists thought that even greater developments might be just around the corner and that room temperature superconductivity might soon be a reality.

After much discussion, however, designers of the SSC have decided not to wait for development of new superconducting materials but to use the helium-cooled magnets originally planned. The scientific and political factors on which this decision was based are discussed in Chapter Seven.

Physicists have had to design two major types of

magnets for the SSC. The first type, a dipole, will perform the task of bending the proton beams as they travel around the accelerator ring. The second type, a quadrupole, is used to focus the beam.

Remember that the beam consists of many protons, all of which carry a positive electrical charge. Repulsion among these like-charged protons will tend to cause the beam to diverge or "smear out." Smearing out also occurs because of errors in injecting particles and in the magnetic fields within the ring. The job of the quadrupole magnets will be to push the protons back together into a tight beam.

The ring will also contain other magnets with specialized functions. Some, for example, will make corrections in the beam to "fine-tune" the control of the dipoles and quadrupoles. Others are needed to change the path of the beams so that they will collide with each other in the interaction halls.

Of the 10,104 magnets in the main ring, 3,840 will be dipoles; 888, quadrupoles; and the remaining 5,376, special purpose magnets. Each dipole will be 17.34 meters (56.88 feet) long and weigh 6,759 kilograms (14,900 pounds), while each quadrupole will be 4.32 meters (14.2 feet) long and weigh 1,114 kilograms (2,456 pounds). The total weight of all magnets together will be 41,500 tons and will require 19,400 kilometers (12,000 miles) of superconducting cable.[31]

Cooling for the superconducting wires will come from ten refrigerating units placed uniformly around the ring. Each unit will maintain liquid helium at $-269°C$ ($-452°F$) inside a jacket of liquid nitrogen at $-196°C$ ($-321°F$).

Particle collisions • Protons for the SSC will be produced by the ionization of hydrogen gas. After acceleration in the linac and the low-, medium-, and high-energy booster synchrotrons, the proton beam will be split into two parts as it enters the main ring. One beam will circulate in a clockwise direction; the other, in a counterclockwise direction.

On their trips around the main ring, the protons will have their energy boosted from 1 TeV to 20 TeV. The accelerating sections needed to provide this additional energy are very efficient and take up only 23 meters (75 feet) of the 83-kilometer-long ring.

After 15 minutes in the main ring, the protons will have traveled three million times around the ring and have reached their maximum energy. At this point, each beam will be about 0.2 millimeter in diameter and consist of proton bunches about 15 centimeters long and 10 micrometers in diameter. Each bunch will carry about ten billion protons.

Collisions will take place within one of the interaction halls, where deflecting magnets will cause the two opposing beams to intersect with each other. The idea of a "collision" may need some explanation. The event does not compare, for example, to the collision of two cars— a sudden crash in which both cars are demolished. Remember that the beams consist of bunches of protons, about ten billion protons to the bunch. That may seem like a very crowded bunch, but protons are very small. Each bunch of protons actually consists primarily of empty space. Thus, when two bunches collide, more than anything else, they simply pass through each other. Probably no more than about 1 percent of the protons—about a hundred million of them—will collide in any one second.

Of course, a hundred million collisions is still a great many events. But the vast majority of protons are unaffected by their passage through the interaction hall. They can travel back into the main ring and continue on their paths around the ring.

This process is so efficient that proton beams can remain in the main ring for up to two days without being replenished. During their 53,600,000,000-kilometer (33,500,000,000-mile) trip during this time, the proton bunches will never vary by more than about 1 millimeter (0.04 inch) in width!

Finding out what happens during particle collisions will be difficult. Of the one hundred million expected events, more than 99.9 percent will be of no interest. They will result in familiar, well-studied particles and events. The main task of the SSC's detection system, then, will be to screen out uninteresting events and throw out familiar data. This task can certainly be compared to the proverbial search for a needle in a haystack.

To accomplish this end, the SSC will make use of traditional detection devices such as calorimeters and bubble chambers. The major difference from other accelerator detection systems will be high-speed computers needed to examine each event and decide whether it is worth studying in more detail. Each detector will be divided into many pie-shaped segments, each with its own individual computers. The data from all the individual smaller computers will then be fed into a larger mainframe machine for further analysis. Out of these millions and millions of events, physicists hope, one, two, or a half-dozen will emerge that will tell them more about the structure of quarks, the Higgs boson, the unification of forces, or some other question for which the massive SSC was designed.

CHAPTER SEVEN

THE SSC: CONFLICT AND CONTROVERSY

So who needs yet another particle accelerator? Do we really need to spend billions of dollars on an SSC? The answer to that question is that no one "needs" an SSC the way we need enough food to feed the world's population or the way we need to find a cure for AIDS.

But humans have always felt needs beyond those of survival. Among these intellectual demands has been the desire—the "need"—to better understand the world around us. In fact, one of the qualities which seems to make humans different from other animals is our ability to wonder, to ask why, even when those questions have nothing to do with staying alive.

The historical development of the science we call astronomy, for example, contains a strong element of pure curiosity. Learning about the composition of stars and the structure of galaxies probably has little practical effect on the way humans live their daily lives. Yet, studies like these have been an important part of most human cultures for hundreds of years. Even in twentieth-century America, a society obsessed with practical results and a fair return on the dollar, we were willing to spend billions of dollars to send people to the moon, not because we needed the information to improve our daily lives, but just because we wanted—"needed"—to know more about the world around us.

Physicists' hopes for the SSC have often been phrased in these terms. Our exploration of the nature of matter must continue, they say, simply because there is still more to learn. We have to answer the next set of questions about quarks, leptons, and the fundamental forces simply because the questions have been asked.

It's unfortunate that the cost of this research is so great. But that cannot be a reason for giving up the search, they argue. One statement that reflects this position has put it this way:

> *The scientists who seek the basic rules of the physical world do so out of their own intellectual curiosity, and also as emissaries of a civilization that adheres to the rational view of nature, the belief that the universe is comprehensible through experiment and reason. The goal of high energy physics is to discover the fundamental laws that govern the universe. Doing so shapes our conceptions of our own world and its place in the cosmos. The better we understand where we came from the more chance we have of controlling where we are going. The SSC is an instrument for the pursuit of this age-old goal.* [32]

The practical benefits of the SSC • Selling an expensive project like the SSC to government officials and the general public purely on this basis, the advance of knowledge, is usually difficult, however. Consequently, scientists often look for other ways of justifying a multi-billion-dollar project like the SSC. In a press release about the SSC, for example, the Department of Energy (DOE) claimed that "past investments in studies of the interior of atoms have been repaid hundreds of times over in terms of new knowledge, new technologies, new jobs, national security, advances in medicine, and financial returns to the Treasury."[33]

Alvin W. Trivelpiece, of DOE, noted that the Department's presentation of the SSC concept to President Reagan was couched in terms of such practical benefits to human society. He pointed out to the president that "a third of our GNP [gross national product] owes its existence to atomic physics, and a good fraction of that knowledge came from the accelerator field.[34] The Department did not raise the point about advancing human knowledge because, Trivelpiece thought, that argument "would have been undignified."

SSC supporters believe that many benefits will accrue not only from collider research, but also from the design and construction of the giant machine. According to some scientists, low-temperature studies, magnet technology and metallurgy are already benefiting from research on the SSC.

Pride and profit • Yet a third argument for the SSC has centered on national pride. Americans (not alone in the world) have an intense desire to avoid being second-best in almost anything: nuclear bombs, the space race, hockey, or particle physics. It's hardly surprising, then, to hear proponents of the SSC reminding the nation of the dangers of falling behind the Russians, the Japanese, or the West Europeans by not building the new machine. Representative Robert Roe of New Jersey called on this argument in a speech before Congress when he claimed that the SSC "can serve as a beginning of our nation's recovery as the world leader in science and technology."[35]

Scientists themselves are keenly aware of this argument. Dr. Leon Lederman, director of Fermilab, has pointed out that "it is very important that we be among the world's leaders in this area."[36] SSC supporters also point out the danger of *not* remaining a world leader in particle physics. For example, California's Representative Ron Packwood warned that "if Congress fails to fund this machine, we may as well begin preparing a couple of thousand visas for our most outstanding physicists."[37]

In fact, the president's decision in early 1987 to support the SSC seems to have been largely a matter of national pride. Secretary of the Department of Energy John Herrington confirmed that the president's decision "reflects a desire to maintain U.S. lead in high energy physics . . . [and is] another clear sign that President Reagan is committed to keeping this nation on the cutting edge of world leadership and competitiveness."[38]

The statement of a highly respected physicist, Nobel Prize winner Dr. James W. Cronin, illustrates how one can combine all of these arguments in a single statement of support for the SSC. He has written that the SCC *should proceed for the simple reason that the exploration and understanding of nature have consistently advanced civilization and are one of its prime features. Discoveries made in the course of fundamental scientific investigations have in time led to new technologies which have profoundly affected life on this planet. . . . The intellectual achievements of humanity in its relatively brief time on earth are almost beyond belief. Furthermore, they are among the most positive aspects of human nature. The spirit of a nation and the pride of its people can only be enhanced when science, including the exploration of our planet, solar system, galaxy and universe, is among its highest priorities.* [39]

A final argument in support of the SSC is economic. The argument is based on the rather simple fact that construction and operation of the new accelerator will be one of the largest (if not *the* largest) scientific projects in human history.

The SSC is expected to cost $4 billion to build and to employ forty-five hundred workers during the eight years of construction. After completion, the accelerator complex will have an annual budget of $270 million, employ a full-time staff of twenty-five hundred, and provide facilities for about five hundred visiting scientists. The machine is expected to provide a giant economic impetus to the state in which it is located. [40] For many government officials, politicians, business people, industrialists, in fact, the scientific features of the SSC are secondary to the economic bonanza it represents.

Real and imagined benefits • Enthusiasm for the SSC is far from universal. From its earliest conception, the accelerator project has had its critics from both inside and outside of science. For example, some critics question the supposed benefits to be gained from SSC research. Few scientists doubt the value of the SSC for basic particle physics research. But hopes for practical benefits seem remote and unrealistic to some observers. Dr. James Krumhansl, professor of physics at Cornell University and vice president of the American Physical Society, has argued that "in the last 30 years I have not seen that particle physics has made any substantive contribution to technology generally, nor energy science and technology specifically. The proposed project will not be different. This investment will do nothing, either, to improve our scientific, technological, or industrial competitiveness."[41] And Leon Lederman, director of Fermilab, has said, flat-out, "You would never build an accelerator to glean indirect [that is, practical] benefits."[42]

Limited resources and scientific competition • Perhaps the most commonly voiced and most obvious question is where the money for the accelerator is coming from. Some observers were amazed that an administration that had called for budgetary restraint for seven years gave its approval to such an expensive project.

President Reagan did not himself presume to answer that question. He authorized the project and pledged that money would not come from other science projects to support it. But he made no suggestions as to where Congress might find funds for the accelerator's multi-billion-dollar costs.

For scientists, the issue is not even as simple as hoping that Congress will know where to find the SSC money. Many of them fear that, the president's pledge notwithstanding, money will come out of other research budgets. The SSC can be funded, they fear, only by cutting back on other types of scientific research.

Philip W. Anderson, professor of physics at Princeton University and Nobel laureate, has talked about this issue, and about the reasons it hasn't reached the news media. He says: "The [scientists] do not want to be seen as opposing research—maybe the next one to go would be your own favorite. But I think if you were taking a secret ballot among scientists you would find that only a very small number favored the supercollider."[43]

As final decisions on the SSC approached, some scientists became more vocal on this issue. For example, Dr. Arno Penzias, Nobel laureate and vice president for research at Bell Laboratories, claimed that "small science groups, which train the next generation of scientists, are getting squeezed." He expressed the view that the money spent on the SSC could be used more productively if spread out over many projects.[44] Perhaps the strongest statement to appear in print came from Dr. Rustum Roy of Pennsylvania State University, who said that the SSC was "a supertoy for a tiny fraction of the spoiled brats of the engineering and science community."[45]

Supporters of the SSC have tried to defuse this issue. Dr. Maury Tigner, Anderson's professional colleague and a member of the SSC Central Design Group, has responded by promising that "none of us for one moment would want to press on with this great wave of discovery in particle physics if it were to come out of the hides of other scientists. We may be parochial in certain respects, but we have a deep respect for science as an entity; to make a huge advance in one part of it at the expense of others would be a bad mistake."[46] Tigner further points out that the administration has promised a doubling of the National Science Foundation (NSF) budget in the next five years. That increase should guarantee that worthy research will not go unfunded, he believes.

Yet, funding for the SSC inevitably raises serious economic questions in a time of dramatic federal deficits and uncertain economic conditions. Already the necessity of making choices in the funding of physics projects has become obvious. Financial belt-tightening in late 1987, partly in anticipation of SSC expenses, was responsible for the shutdown of two accelerators at SLAC and the reduction in research at Fermilab.[47]

The SSC as a "quark-barrel" project • Some observers also worry about the economics and politics of the SSC. They acknowledge the widespread and enthusiastic support of legislators and many in the general public early in the project's history. But they attribute at least a part of that support to a hope that their own states and communities would get "a piece of the action." As Representative Dave McCurdy of Oklahoma has observed, "It's becoming like a national lottery. Everybody's trying to get a piece."[48] One cynic has even labeled the SSC concept a giant "quark-barrel" project.[49]

Representative Don Ritter of Pennsylvania argues that support for the SSC crested early, before a site for the accelerator had been chosen. He predicted, however, that, as states were eliminated from consideration, support would wane and that "many SSC supporters will desert ship."[50]

To some legislators the whole economic argument for the SSC simply didn't hold water. Hard economic data do not exist, they said, to support the position that the SSC will be a great boon to the state in which it's located. Explaining his reason for opposing the state's bid to build the SSC in California, State Assemblyman Phil Isenberg claimed that "this is the boondoggle to end all boondoggles, and we're mindlessly willing to give away the store to get it. We want it because Texas or Illinois wants it. The question that was conveniently ignored in all the controversy was the cost to the taxpayers and whether it's worth it. I think the answer is no."[51]

To wait or not to wait • A final objection to the SSC—at least to plans to begin working on it now—has surfaced from an unexpected direction: progress in research on superconductivity. By 1988, scientists were discovering materials that are superconductive at temperatures near the boiling point of nitrogen. To some scientists, these discoveries were highly relevant to the design of the SSC. They meant that the high cost of maintaining the SSC magnets at the temperature of liquid helium might be bypassed. They proposed a delay in the design and construction of the new accelerator until the benefits of the latest discoveries could be assessed.

Some writers worried that new superconducting materials would make the SSC obsolete even before it was built. *The New York Times* weighed in with its own opinion in an April 28, 1987 editorial asking for a delay in further work on the project until the significance of superconducting research on the machine had been determined.[52]

Physicists involved with the SSC project have been less than enthusiastic about these suggestions. They argue that savings from the new superconducting materials would be much less—they estimate 5 to 10 percent—than most people imagine.[53] Besides, they point out, the new superconducting materials are not metals, but glass-like ceramics. No one can predict how long it will be before such materials can be processed and fabricated for use in electromagnets.

Finally, particle physicists worry that any delay in the SSC project at this point could be disastrous. Fueled by President Reagan's 1987 approval of the machine, everyone connected with the SSC is riding a wave of optimism. To hesitate now, especially for a savings of only 5 percent, might result in a critical loss of momentum, they say.

The decision to build • While debate over the SSC continues, planning for the new machine goes forward. In November of 1988, Energy Secretary Herrington announced that Texas had been chosen as the location for the SSC. A 16,000-acre site near Waxahachie, south of Dallas, had been selected over possible sites in six other states. Texans were ecstatic, both with the scientific prestige and with the two thousand high-tech jobs and $270 million annual payroll the SSC would bring the state.

Enthusiasm for the decision was not unanimous, however. Representatives from the six losing states (Arizona, Colorado, Illinois, Michigan, North Carolina, and

Tennessee) accused Secretary Herrington of playing politics with the SSC decision, and some requested an independent review of his choice.

Even at this late stage, controversy over the giant particle accelerator had not diminished. On the one hand, SSC designers see the culmination of sixty years of research at hand. Crucial discoveries seem just around the corner. Particle physics is at a turning point before which no one in the field wants to pause or turn back.

But what price should we pay for the machine? Can our deficit-ridden economy support a project of this magnitude? Can we ensure that other fields of science obtain the funding that they too deserve and need? Whatever its future, the SSC seems destined to be a machine that raises difficult questions, both in science and in the general society.

SOURCE NOTES

1 *To the Heart of the Matter—The Superconducting Super Collider* (Washington: Universities Research Association, 1987), p. 23.
2 Ibid.
3 All statistical data on accelerators at the SLAC are obtained from published press releases from SLAC.
4 For the early history of the cyclotron, see M. S. Livingston, "History of the Cyclotron. Part I," and E. M. McMillan, "History of the Cyclotron. Part II," pp. 261–278, in R. Bruce Lindsay, *Energy in Atomic Physics, 1925–1960* (Stroudsburg, PA: Hutchinson Ross, 1983).
5 M. Stanley Livingston and John P. Blewett, *Particle Accelerators* (New York: McGraw-Hill, 1962), p. 188.
6 Livingston and Blewett, p. 354.
7 Livingston and Blewett, p. 367.
8 Franklin Miller, Jr., *College Physics* (New York: Harcourt Brace Jovanovich, 1982), p. 797.
9 *The Encyclopedia Americana* (Danbury, CT: Grolier, 1986), vol. 21, p. 494.
10 Livingston and Blewett, p. 635.
11 Yuval Ne'eman and Yoram Kirsh, *The Particle Hunters* (Cambridge: Cambridge University Press, 1986), p. 189.
12 All statistical data on accelerators at Fermilab are obtained from published press releases from the Fermi National Accelerator Laboratory.

13 All statistical data on CERN accelerators are from published press releases from the Centre Européen pour la Recherche Nucléaire.
14 Ne'eman and Kirsh, p. 222.
15 Gale Cook, "The Last Living Dinosaur," *Image* magazine of the San Francisco *Examiner*, July 12, 1987, pp. 8–9.
16 Herman Winick, "Synchrotron Radiation," *Scientific American*, November 1987, p. 91.
17 Ibid., p. 88.
18 M. Mitchell Waldrop, "Why Go To 20 TeV?" *Science*, July 25, 1986, p. 422.
19 Sheldon L. Glashow and Leon M. Lederman, "The SSC: A Machine for the Nineties," *Physics Today*, March 1985, p. 31.
20 A. Appelquist, M. K. Gaillard, and J. D. Jackson, "Physics at the Superconducting Super Collider," *American Scientist*, March-April 1984, p. 152.
21 Martinus J. G. Veltman, "The Higgs Boson," *Scientific American*, November 1986, p. 76.
22 Ibid.
23 Chris Quigg and Roy F. Schwitters, "Elementary Particle Physics and the Superconducting Super Collider," *Science*, March 28, 1986, p. 1524.
24 Veltman, p. 84.
25 See, for example, the discussion in Quigg and Schwitters, pp. 1525–1527.
26 M. Mitchell Waldrop, "In Search of Dark Matter," *Science*, October 10, 1986, p. 152.
27 *To the Heart of the Matter*, pp. 18–19.
28 All statistical data on the SSC comes from *To the Heart of the Matter* and J. David Jackson, Maury Tigner, and Stanley Wojcicki, "The Superconducting Super Collider," *Scientific American*, March 1986, pp. 66–77.
29 *The 1988 Information Please Almanac* (Boston: Houghton Mifflin, 1988), p. 384.
30 Jackson, Tigner and Wojcicki, p. 74.
31 *To the Heart of the Matter*, p. 23.
32 *To the Heart of the Matter*, p. 38.
33 Robert Bazell, "Quark Barrel Politics," *New Republic*, June 22, 1987, p. 10.
34 William D. Marbach, "When Protons—and Politics—Collide," *Newsweek*, July 6, 1987, p. 45.
35 Mark Crawford, "Supercollider Faces Budget Barrier," *Science*, April 17, 1987, p. 246.
36 Ibid.
37 Marbach, p. 44.

38 Robert E. Taylor, "President Will Request Funds to Build World's Largest Particle Accelerator," *Wall Street Journal,* February 2, 1987, p. 14.

39 James W. Cronin, "The Case for the Supercollider," *Bulletin of the Atomic Scientists,* May 1986, p. 10.

40 Robert Reinhold, "Physics, Schmysics — This Project Is a $6 Billion Plum," *New York Times,* March 29, 1987, p. E4.

41 Bazell, p. 10.

42 Marbach, p. 45.

43 James Gleick, "Advances Pose Obstacle to Atom Smasher Plan," *New York Times,* April 14, 1987, p. C6.

44 David Stipp, "Federal Plan to Delve into Subatomic Matter Draws Fire over Costs," *Wall Street Journal,* January 5, 1988, p. 1.

45 Ibid.

46 Arthur Fisher, "The World's Biggest Machine," *Popular Science,* June 1987, p. 110.

47 Stipp, p. 12.

48 Marbach, p. 44.

49 Bazell, p. 9.

50 Stipp, p. 12.

51 Steve Wiegand, "State's Unusual Collider Offer," San Francisco *Chronicle,* September 7, 1987, p. 1.

52 *New York Times,* April 28, 1987, p. A30.

53 Gleick, p. C6.

BIBLIOGRAPHY

Apfel, Necia H. *It's All Elementary: From Atoms to the Quantum World of Quarks, Leptons, and Gluons.* New York: Lothrop, Lee & Shepard, 1985. A review of the history of quantum theory, of newly discovered subatomic particles, and recent developments in theories about the origin of the universe.

Appelquist, A.; M.K. Gaillard; and J. D. Jackson. "Physics at the Superconducting Super Collider." *American Scientist,* March/April 1984, 151–155. A clear explanation of the reasons the SSC is needed, with a description of the proposed accelerator.

Boslough, John. "Worlds within atoms." *National Geographic,* May 1985, 634–663. In usual *Geographic* style, this article is written with great charm and illustrated with magnificent photos and drawings. An excellent introduction for the amateur.

Chester, Michael. *Particles: An Introduction to Particle Physics.* New York: Macmillan, 1978. An older book that describes the history of atomic theory followed by a review of recent developments in particle physics.

Engdahl, Sylvia, and Rick Robertson. *The Sub-nuclear Zoo: New Discoveries in High Energy Physics.* New York: Atheneum, 1977. The discoveries are no longer so new, but the background information provided in this book is useful and well presented.

Fritzsch, Harald. *Quarks: The Stuff of Matter.* New York: Basic Books, 1983. This book presents information on the Standard Model about as clearly as any.

Glashow, Sheldon L., and Leon M. Lederman. "The SSC: A machine for the nineties." *Physics Today,* March 1985, 28–37. A comprehensive, somewhat technical article describing the needs for the SSC along with a description of the machine.

Harari, Haim. "The structure of quarks and leptons." *Scientific American,* April 1983, 56–68. A thorough explanation of the Standard Model.

Hughes, I. S. *Elementary Particles,* 2d ed. Cambridge: Cambridge University Press, 1985. A challenging book that provides all you need to know about particle physics.

Jackson, J. David; Maury Tigner; and Stanley Wojcicki. "The Superconducting Super Collider." *Scientific American,* March 1986, 66–77. One of the best articles to tie together the gaps in the Standard Model that make the SSC so necessary.

Livingston, M. Stanley, and John P. Blewett. *Particle Accelerators.* New York: McGraw-Hill, 1962. Although an older book, this text provides a great deal of detailed information about accelerators. Much is beyond the level of beginning readers, but enough understandable information is included to make it worth looking at.

Ne'eman, Yuval, and Yoram Kirsh. *The Particle Hunters.* Cambridge: Cambridge University Press, 1986. The emphasis in this book is on the theories of particle physics, but some valuable background on particle accelerators is also included.

Quigg, Chris. "Elementary particles and forces." *Scientific American,* April 1985, 84–95. A good, but fairly difficult discussion of the Standard Model.

————, and Roy F. Schwitters, "Elementary particle physics and the Superconducting Super Collider." *Science,* March 28, 1986, 1522–1527. A detailed explanation of the theoretical reasons that the SSC is needed now.

Ratner, B. S. *Accelerators of Charged Particles.* Oxford: Pergamon Press, 1964. An older book, translated from the Russian, but a good introduction to some fundamental ideas.

Stwertka, Albert. *Recent Revolutions in Physics*. New York: Franklin Watts, 1985. A book about accelerators and the particles they have discovered and produced.

Sutton, Christine. "Ninety years around the atom." *New Scientist*, January 8, 1985, 49–53. A well-written, brief history of particle research with some outstanding photographs.

Taubes, Gary. "Collision on the super collider." *Discover*, July 1985, 60–69. A very well-written article that clearly explains why the SSC is needed and how the idea has been developed over the past decade.

———. "Is anything left out there?" *Discover*, April 1987, 42–58. Not specifically about the SSC, but a wonderful introduction to the social, psychological, and political aspects of particle-hunting.

Trefil, James S. *From Atoms to Quarks*. New York: Scribner, 1980. A somewhat dated but very nice attempt to explain particle physics to younger readers.

Waldrop, M. Mitchell. "Decision time for the Super Collider." *Science*, July 25, 1986, 420–423. A valuable article because of the historical background it provides on the SSC project.

Weinberg, Steven. *The Discovery of Subatomic Particles*. San Francisco: W. H. Freeman, 1983. A nice review of the history of the discovery of subatomic particles.

———. *The First Three Minutes*. New York: Basic Books, 1977. For those who are interested in seeing what scientists think the first three minutes of creation might have looked like, with a hint as to what the SSC will add to this story.

Winick, Herman. "Synchrotron radiation." *Scientific American*, November 1987, 88–89. A good description of the way synchrotron radiation is produced and how it is being used in science and technology.

INDEX

Frequency, of machine, 43–44
Frequency-modulated (FM) cyclotron. *See* Synchrocyclotron
Frequency of oscillation, 36

Gauge particles, 76
Generations, 71
Glass, 32
Gluons, 75, 76
Gravitational force, 15, 74–76, 86
Gravitons, 75, 76

Hadrons, 74, 85, 91
Helium, 13, 29, 101, 102, 114
Herrington, John, 109, 115–116
Higgs, Peter W., 88
Higgs boson, 88, 89, 90–91, 92, 105
Higgs field, 90
Hydrogen, 20, 29, 30, 32, 103

Ionization, 29, 30, 32
Ions, positively charged, 29
Isenberg, Phil, 114
Isotopes, radioactive, 64, 78, 79–80

J/psi, 29

Kaons, 15
Krumhansl, James, 111

Large Electron-Positron (LEP) collider, 60
Laser beams, for aligning linear accelerators, 27
Lawrence, Ernest O., 11, 44; his cyclotron, 12, 13, 14, 19, 39–40
Lederman, Leon, 109, 111
LEP. *See* Large Electron-Positron collider

Leptons, 71–72, 75, 85–86, 94–95, 107
Light, 24, 32, 41, 47–48, 67–68, 76
Light microscopes, 67, 68
Linacs. *See* Linear accelerators
Linear accelerators, 12–13, 19–20, *21*, 22–33, 46–48; Cockroft-Walton accelerator, 12–14, 19; disadvantages, 34, 52; electron linacs, 24–25, 50, 73, 78–79; feeder machine for Tevatron, 54; proton linacs, 23–25, 39; and SSC, 98, 103; in Stanford Linear Accelerator Center, 25
Lithium metal, 12–13
Livingston, M. Stanley, 11, 40

McCurdy, Dave (U.S. Rep.), 113
Magnets and magnetic fields, 30, 51, 52, 89–91; accelerator magnets of SSC, 98–100, 115; in cyclotrons, 34, *35*, 36–39, 41; in sector-focusing cyclotrons, 45–46, 48; superconducting magnets, 59, 100–102; in synchrocyclotrons, 49; in synchrotrons, 48, 49; and Tevatron, 44, *58*, 59
Mass, 14, 30, 34, 41, 87; relationship with energy, 68–69, 76, 85, 90, 92; relativistic increases, 41–45, 49
Matter, structure of, 15, 68, 91, 92
Mediating particles, 76
Medical therapy, 79, 81, 108
Midwest Institute for Neutron Therapy (MINT), 79
Mirror symmetry, 91
Multiwire counters, 32
Muon neutrinos, 71–72

Muons, 71–72

National Research Council, 40
National Science Foundation
(NSF), 113
Neutrinos, 62, 91
Neutrons, 12, 18, 66–67, 73, 79;
as compound particles, 76, 85–
86, 94
New York Times, The, 114–115
Nitrogen, 101, 102, 114
Nobel Institute, 40
Nobel Prize winners, 62, 109–
110, 112
Nuclei, 11–13, 17–18, 66, 74–75;
and radioactive materials, 80;
subatomic particles produced,
15, 62, 68, 95

Oak Ridge National Laboratory,
40

Parkwood, Ron (U.S. Rep.), 109
Particle acceleration, 17, *31,* 65,
69–71, 74
Particle detectors, 29–33
Particle physics, 62, 69–71, 74,
76, 84
Penzias, Arno, 112
PEP (ring), 27
Phasotron (Soviet Union). *See*
Synchrocyclotron
Photons, 75, 76, 89
Pions, 15, 62; neutral, 69
Plates, charged, 17–18
Positrons, 18, 27, 53, 60, 91
Pressure, applied in bubble cham-
bers, 29–30
Propane, liquid, 29
Protons, 12–13, 16, 18, 20, 22–
25; age estimation of docu-
ments, 80–81; beam energy,
53, 79; beams, 59, 98; beams

in synchrocyclotrons, 45; as
compound particles, 67, 73–74,
94; discovery of, 12, 66; effect
of an increase in mass, 41–45;
and electromagnetic force, 76;
in a cyclotron, 34–36, 38, *39,*
40; mass of, 41, 68, 90; and
medical therapy, 79; "out of
phase," 24, 44; proton-antiproton collisions, 62; and radioactive materials, 79–80; in SSC,
98, 102–104; and strong force,
75, 76; in a synchrotron, 47,
49–51, 62; used in the Tevatron, 54, 59
Psi, 29

Quadrupoles, 102
Quarks, 67, 71–76, 85–86, 91,
94–95; structure of, 105, 107

Reagan, Ronald, 108, 111, 115
Reflection, 67
Rings, 16, 27, 53; PEP, 27;
SPEAR, 27; SSC, 96–98, 102–
104; synchrotron, 48–49, 51,
54; Tevatron, 59, 96
Ritter, Don (U.S. Rep.), 113–114
Roe, Robert (U.S. Rep.), 109
Roy, Rustum, 112
Rubbia, Carlo, 62
Rutherford, Ernest, 12, 74

Sector-focusing, 46
Sigma zero, 74
SLAC. *See* Stanford Linear Accel-
erator Center
SLC. *See* Stanford Linear Acceler-
ator Center, Linear Collider
Spark chambers, 32, 33
SPEAR (collider), 27
SSC. *See* Superconducting Super
Collider

Standard Model theory, 15, 16, 70–71, 74, 76–77; and development of SSC, 85, 87, 88

Stanford Linear Accelerator Center (SLAC), 25, *26*, 27, *28*, 29; internal structure of protons and neutrons, 73–74; Linear Collider (SLC), 29; no major breakthroughs expected, 84; research frontier for particle physics, 54; two accelerators shut down in 1987, 113; two-gluon particles, 76

Strong force, 15, 74–76, 86, 88

Superconducting Super Collider (SSC), 16, 53, 59, 72, 84–95; accelerator-beam energy to be produced, 19; controversy due to expense, 106–116; design of, 96, *97*, 98, *99*, 100–105; and Standard Model theory, 77

Superconductivity, 59, 100–102, 114–115

Synchrocylotrons, 41–45, 49; CERN's first accelerator (SC), 60, 62–64

Synchrotrons, 46, *47*, 48–54, *55*, 59–60; booster, 54; CERN, 59–60; CERN's proton synchrotron (PS), 62, *63;* CERN's super proton synchrotron (SPS), *61*, 62, *63;* electron, 81, 83; radiation emitted, 49–53, 81–83; radiation used to treat diseases, 49–50; and SSC, 98, 103; world's major ones, 50

Tau, 71–72

Tau leptons, 29

Tau neutrinos, 71–72

Tevatron. *See* Fermilab

Thomas, Llewellyn H., 46

Tigner, Maury, 112–113

Trivelpiece, Alvin W., 108

Universities Research Association, 16

Vacuum, 25, 32

Van der Meer, Simon, 62

Velocity, determined by "footprint" in a bubble chamber, 30, 33; determining circle radius in a cyclotron, 34, 36, 38; law of conservation of momentum, 52; and mass of a particle, 41; related to energy, 18

Walton, E.T.S., 12

Water, and Cherenkov radiation, 32

Wavelengths, 67–68, 73; and age estimation of documents, 80–81; of synchrotron radiation, 82

W bosons, 15, 62, 75–76, 87–90, 95

Weak force, 15, 74–76, 86–87, 91

Xenon, liquid, 29

X rays, 78–79, 80–82

Z bosons, 62, 75–76, 87–90, 95

ABOUT THE AUTHOR

David E. Newton is adjunct professor
in the College of Professional Studies
at the University of San Francisco,
and the author of more than forty books
in the sciences.

He has taught for many years at both
the high school and college level.